STORIES OF
INSPIRATION

Lessons and Laughter
in Student Affairs

SARAH M. MARSHALL, PH.D.
EDITOR

D1010036

NASPA
Student Affairs Administrators
in Higher Education

Additional copies may be purchased by contacting the NASPA publications
department at 301-638-1749 or visiting http://www.naspa.org/publications.

ISBN 0-931654-40-8

STORIES OF
INSPIRATION

NASPA
Student Affairs Administrators
in Higher Education

This book is dedicated to the thousands of student affairs educators who, every day, make a difference in the lives of college students. Thank you for your dedication, passion, and inspiration.

INTRODUCTION

I first had the idea for this book in the late 1990s after I met a student named John. After serving as a hall director, student activities coordinator, and leadership training facilitator, I had accepted a position as an assistant director of residence life for a mid-size private university. The position focused primarily on the nuts-and-bolts operations of residence life—occupancy, budget and revenue projections, facilities management, contracts, building acquisitions, and inventories. I also served as an upper-level conduct officer and liaison to dining services. My mentor encouraged me to accept the position because she felt it was essential for me to learn the operations side of a university. This would be a valuable experience if I ever wanted to be a dean of students. Following my mentor's advice, I took the position, knowing it would be a good career move even though there would be little student interaction—or, should I say, little positive student interaction.

I had loved being on the frontline with students. I enjoyed their curiosity, creativity, energy, and desire to learn both inside and outside the classroom. The students often inspired and motivated me, until I accepted the assistant director position.

I quickly learned that I was the policy enforcer. Because the buck often stopped with me, I received most of the complaints from students and parents. They complained about everything—the size of their rooms, the mismatched furniture, the food, the turnaround time of maintenance requests, the cost, the residency requirement. The list seemed endless. Students often wanted to break their housing or dining contracts or be exempted from the two-year residency requirement. While some of the requests were justified, many were not. I was instructed to release students from their contracts only in extreme cases because if I let one student out, others would follow. Attrition would hurt our budget. Needless to say, many students were very upset when I didn't grant their requests. A pleasing person by nature, I found routinely saying no difficult and taxing.

During this time, I also became frustrated with the university and its limited resources. I, too, had difficulty understanding why we couldn't fix the leaky roof, decrease the occupancy of a one-bedroom apartment from four to three people, or provide different meal options. I often found myself required to defend policies that I didn't believe in, and my suggestions for change were often shot down with the budget "bottom line" defense.

It is difficult for me to admit, but over time, the constant negative interactions with students and frustrations with limited resources started to wear on me. In two short years, I went from loving students to almost hating them. I couldn't understand why they didn't meet deadlines, fill out paperwork correctly, cease the vandalism, or simply stop losing their keys. I knew few students as persons, and those I did were often the troublemakers I met in conduct hearings. My enthusiasm for students and student affairs was replaced with cynicism, contempt, and intolerance.

Shortly after fall opening, I received a telephone message from a student's mother asking me to call her regarding special accommodations for her son. I immediately assumed this would be another parent making unrealistic demands. Since our buildings were in overflow, I jumped to the conclusion that there would be little I could do and braced myself for another "Sorry, but I can't help you" call.

Once I had Mrs. Stevens on the line, I set my cynicism aside as I listened to her son's story:

> Mrs. Marshall, I'm sorry to trouble you during such a busy time, but I felt it was important to talk with you about my son John. John was scheduled to attend your university this fall, but early this summer he became very sick. It has been John's lifelong dream to attend your school. He studied hard and even earned a scholarship. Although his father and I encouraged him to apply to other universities as backups, he only applied to yours. He was a star athlete in high school, an active student leader, and an honor roll student. Despite his positive high school experience, John was very eager to start college.
>
> As I mentioned, this summer John became very ill. He went through a battery of tests while we watched his health deteriorate. The doctors finally determined that his liver was failing. His only hope was a liver transplant. John was placed on the donor list and, two weeks ago, he received a new liver. While we were grateful for the liver, each day John prayed that he would receive one in time to still start classes this fall. While my husband and I knew that was unrealistic, John was devastated when he learned he couldn't start school right away.
>
> He actually had the transplant the same day your classes started. I get very emotional when I think about it. This kid goes through life-threatening surgery, and when he wakes up, the first thing he asks me is, "Mom, has school started yet?" I kissed him and said, "Yes, son it has." As I watched a tear trickle down his cheek, I promised myself that I would do everything possible to make sure that he got to college as soon as physically possible.

Mrs. Stevens had simple requests. John needed a single room beginning spring semester. They also needed early access so she could thoroughly sanitize the room. She reinforced the necessity of each request as his body could reject the organ at any time, and a sanitary environment was essential to ward off infection. I expressed my concern that even though his room might be clean, a residence hall was not the most sanitary environment. I was willing to exempt him from the residency requirement and help them find off-campus housing if they preferred. She quickly declined because John made it perfectly clear that he wanted a true college experience. He was already worried about starting classes midyear. "He just wants to fit in. He wants to make friends, and living on campus is one way to accomplish both." I assured her that we would meet both her requests and any others that she or her son had. I thanked her for her call and arranged a time to speak again.

I hung up the phone, shook my head in disbelief, and wept. In that moment, I realized how removed I had become, how far off-course. Where had the student-loving, optimistic, light-hearted person gone? When had I stopped listening, stopped caring, and stopped trying to help? Where did my compassion for students go? When had my focus shifted away from student needs to my own? While I don't know when exactly I temporarily lost my vision, I do know that one phone call changed my life, helped me find focus, and renewed my spirit.

I will forever be grateful for the powerful lesson that John's mother taught me that day. Her son's dream was to attend our university. Despite incredible obstacles, John remained dedicated to that dream. His story reminded me of the little things that I can do to make a major difference in the life of a student. John's story reinforced an idea I read in an article titled "Behind Every Face Is a Story" by Lee Williams. In it, she reminds us of the importance of knowing our students and listening to their stories. If we don't care enough to learn about them individually, how can we help them? From that point on, I recommitted myself to my profession. I took time to listen to concerns, made judgments based on merit rather than policy, and looked for positive teachable moments in my student interactions.

One Sunday in January, before the start of the spring semester, I met John and his parents and escorted them to his room. I answered their numerous questions, introduced them to John's hall director and resident advisor, and offered to help sanitize his room. If you had met John then, you wouldn't have guessed that he had transplant surgery only months before. You wouldn't have guessed that attending our university was his life's dream. Standing before me, he looked like an average college student wearing an oversized shirt, baggy jeans, and a ball cap to cover his uncombed hair. Typical of most students in the presence of their parents, he was quiet, obviously embarrassed by their questions, and eager to see them leave.

You'd never have guessed the story behind John's face. Over the years, how many stories have we discounted or overlooked? How many life's dreams are we making happen or ignoring? A career in student affairs is filled with its ups and downs, its rewards and its challenges. When life gets busy and I find myself frustrated with my chosen profession, I often think of John and how I helped him achieve his life's goal.

I mentioned earlier that John's story helped serve as my inspiration for this book. I think of student affairs as a heroic profession. Every day we give of ourselves to help others. While student affairs work is often rewarding, there are potentially many "dark clouds," such as long hours; low pay; disrespectful, apathetic, or overextended students; difficult parents; shrinking budgets; and little expressed gratitude. It may be challenging for student affairs professionals to find "silver linings" or positive examples that remind us of our purpose and reinforce our dedication.

Despite the harsh realities associated with student affairs work, a career in student affairs can be very rewarding and worthwhile. Frequently, student affairs educators make a difference in the lives of others. The challenge is knowing whether a difference was made. There are times people say "thank you" or "you really helped me out" or "you changed my life." Sometimes it is right away. Sometimes it is years later. Those moments are precious. Because such positive reinforcements in student affairs can be few and far between, I decided to collect those precious moments and share them with a larger audience. Thus, the purpose of this book is to provide a venue for student affairs educators to share their inspirational and humorous stories, along with lessons they learned.

To this end, I solicited stories from student affairs educators. Stories were collected over the course of a year from all levels and divisions—from undergraduate students to vice presidents. Some stories inspire, motivate, or rejuvenate; others provide comic relief. The common denominator is that they touch the reader in some way. These stories allow us to learn through the experiences of others and challenge us to identify lessons that may improve our practice. They help student affairs professionals find purpose in what we do, reinforce the significant role we play on college campuses, teach us valuable lessons, and sometimes simply help us laugh.

IMPORTANCE OF STORYTELLING

We cannot underestimate the significance of storytelling. We are all storytellers by nature. Human beings live storied lives and storytelling is a fundamental form of human communication (Atkinson, 1998). As Dan McAdams suggests, "We are all tellers of tales. We each seek to provide our scattered and often confusing experiences with a sense of coherence by arranging the episodes of our lives into stories" (1993, p. 11). Each time we tell a story, we learn something new about ourselves. In the process of telling stories, we share important truths, as we see them, and in doing so create vital links with those who participate in the exchange (Atkins, 1998). Storytelling can serve as an important function in our lives. After all, the events of our lives seem to be made up of beginnings, conflicts, and resolutions.

Stories can serve several functions. They help us better understand ourselves by gaining a clearer understanding of our experiences, our feelings about them, and their meanings for us. "What generally happens when we tell a story from our own life is that we increase our working knowledge of ourselves because we discover deeper meaning in our lives through the process of reflecting and putting the events, experiences, and feelings that we had lived into oral expression" (Atkins, 1998, p. 1).

Stories can also affirm, validate, and support our own experiences in relation to others (Atkins, 1998). They help us understand our commonalities with others as well as our differences, in both individual lives and in educational practice. Stories can help create bonds or foster a sense of community. Stories can take us beyond our everyday existence into the lives of others.

Storytelling can also be a powerful teaching and learning tool. Because we often use stories to construct and make meaning, they can be an effective way to reach learners with educational messages. Stories can be effective educational tools because they are often believable, rememberable, and entertaining (Neuhauser, 1993). Telling stories may lead to awakenings and transformations resulting in change in others (Rossiter, 2002). Narratives can provide the opportunity for deepened relations with others, new insights, compassionate judgment, the creation of shared knowledge and meanings that can inform professional practice, or an extended vision of responsibility as a professional (Witherell & Noddings, 1991).

I hope this collection will help educate, provide new insights, serve as a venue for shared knowledge, and inform our professional practice. The stories may affirm or validate the reader's experiences, or they may provide a different perspective. The value of storytelling is limitless. Learn from what these storytellers share and take from them an informed understanding of their experiences.

SOLICITATION AND SELECTION OF STORIES

Stories for this book were solicited in a variety of ways. A call for stories detailing the purpose and submission criteria for the book was distributed. The call was included in NASPA weekly updates, listed on most NASPA and American College Personnel Association (ACPA) group e-mail lists, distributed at NASPA, ACPA, and the Association for the Study of Higher Education (ASHE) national conferences. The call was also in NASPA's *Forum*. Program faculty, senior student affairs officers, and NASPA regional vice presidents were sent the call for stories, requesting that they share the submission criteria with their constituents. Approximately 100 stories were submitted. Each story was reviewed by three evaluators. Stories were evaluated for clarity of purpose, their touching or humorous nature, significance to student affairs, and the quality of writing. Of the 100 submitted, 46 were selected for publication. Stories were selected based on uniqueness and reviewers' feedback. In order to ensure a diverse set of stories, some submissions were declined because of similar storylines or themes. Every effort was used to obtain a diverse group of storytellers in terms of gender, race, number of years in the profession, institutional type, and division of student affairs. While taking these characteristics into consideration, the ultimate goal was to find the most interesting and moving stories possible.

ORGANIZATION OF THE BOOK

There is no correct way to read this book. You can start with the first story and end with the last. You can start at the end and work your way forward. You can randomly read one story at a time. After carefully rereading each story, I decided not to organize them by theme. With the exception of the final three stories, I chose to order the narratives individually because each story has its own message and purpose in the book. Trying to place these entries in prescribed categories seemed to devalue their messages. Additionally, some stories speak of sadness, loss, and overcoming extreme adversity. Rather than group these together, I intentionally scattered them throughout the book and infused the more lighthearted stories among them to help lighten the mood for the reader.

In the final section, I offer four stories that center on the theme "lessons learned." Unlike the other entries and their valuable lessons, these stories do not necessarily inspire or make us laugh. Rather, the authors speak of worthwhile lessons they acquired in their student affairs careers. I decided to include these in a separate section because the authors transmit messages that I believe are important for others to hear.

What you are about to read are the personal accounts of 43 individuals telling 46 stories. Stories are heart-warming, inspirational, informative, and funny. Some are based on extraordinary events such as a student's death or a campus crisis. Others are based in the day-to-day interactions student affairs educators have with students during conduct hearings, advising appointments, and impromptu meetings. There also are light-hearted stories detailing student antics and times when student affairs professionals point out their own foibles. Different stories touch people in different ways. You may be particularly moved by one story, only to find that a colleague preferred another. My goal is that you will value those that touch you in some way.

Contributors varied by gender, race, years of experience, institutional types, divisions within student affairs, and number of years in and connection to student affairs. Recent graduates, master's students, new professionals, mid-career professionals, senior-level colleagues, and preparation faculty are represented among the authors.

As you read these stories, some will nicely fit into what some label "traditional" student affairs and others may not. I challenge you, like I did myself, to examine how we define student affairs. Is it by function, title, service, or connection to students? Keep in mind that student affairs divisions are defined differently and reporting structures vary from institution to institution. For the purpose of this book, I broadened my personal definition to include any story related to students, student life, or campus culture.

In *Stories of Inspiration*, you will find stories relating to residence life and student conduct, student activities and student organization advisement, minority student services, orientation, counseling services, and academic advising. You will also find other stories that detail personal experiences and awakenings that are connected to student affairs or higher education.

Some stories in this book are based on extraordinary events, some stem from tragedy, while others emerge from everyday encounters with students. For instance, Peggy Holzweiss tells of her experiences with the bonfire collapse at Texas A&M. Bob Crow and Gail Short Hanson find hope after bomb scares on their campuses in the aftermath of the September 11 terrorist attacks. Janet Walbert, Lee Bird, William Bynum, and Mindy Michels learned from the lost lives of students and colleagues. Others like Becca Minton, Melinda Manning, and Heath Huber impart valuable lessons acquired from survivors of sexual assault. These are powerful stories of individuals overcoming adversity. Another set of stories in this book is based on simple, day-to-day interactions with students and parents. These stories remind us that each day and each interaction can make a difference.

Last, the humorous stories are included to make you smile. These are silly stories that help remind us not to take ourselves too seriously.

In the end, my hope is that this book helps rejuvenate those who have been in the field for some time as well as inspire others who are early in their careers. May graduate students and vice presidents alike enjoy these stories, learn from them, and feel renewed after reading them. This book is intended to provide a positive, inspirational, and sometimes humorous outlook on the profession while reinforcing the significance of student affairs work. I hope these stories touch you in some way and that you find yourself renewed, wiser, or smiling as a result of reading them. Enjoy!

SARAH MARSHALL

References

Atkinson, P. (1998). The life story interview. *Qualitative Research Methods Series,* Vol. 44. Thousand Oaks, CA: Sage Publications.

McAdams, D. (1993). *Stories we live by: Personal myths and the making of the self.* New York: William Morrow.

Neuhauser, P. C. (1993). *Corporate legends and lore: The power of storytelling as a management tool.* New York: McGraw-Hill.

Rossiter, M. (2002). *Narrative and stories in adult teaching and learning.* Columbus, OH: ERIC Clearinghouse on Adult Career and Vocational Education. (ERIC Document Reproduction Service No. ED473147)

Williams, L. B. (1998). Behind every face is a story. *About Campus,* 3(1), 16-21.

Witherell, C., & Noddings, N. (1991). *Stories lives tell: Narrative and dialogue in education.* New York: Teachers College Press.

WHITE MEN CAN MAKE SWEET POTATO PIE

BY
HEATH P. BOICE-PARDEE

I could feel the beads of sweat forming on my brow as they stared at me, on the verge of laughter. In one simple moment, I was reduced to a seventh grader who had gotten up the guts to ask the homecoming queen to the dance, only to be rejected. I didn't think that I said anything funny. All I had said was, "I will make the sweet potato pie for the Thanksgiving food sale." Given the students' reactions, that was enough.

I must admit that a month earlier, I was honored when the student gospel choir had asked me to be their administrative advisor. As a white man, I was also surprised. I liked gospel music, had even listened to it once or twice, but what did I know about advising a gospel choir? The closest thing I had ever come to gospel music was watching Sister Act (which I didn't think counted). But Jamilah, a student with whom I had become acquainted and the leader of the soon-to-be-formed choir assured me, "We don't need an expert in singing. That's what we know. We need help with getting through all the red tape. I can't think of anyone better." I realized that while I was deficient in soul, I excelled in red tape navigation. So I agreed. But when I arrived to the group's first meeting, perky and ready for my new role as advisor, I had second thoughts.

I walked into the meeting room smiling, looking for my sole connection, Jamilah. Much to my dismay, she was absent. When I entered, conversations stopped, and all eyes were on me. As I introduced myself, I noticed that the members of the soon-to-be-gospel-choir gave each other uneasy looks. At least we were all uneasy—perhaps we could develop some camaraderie from that. I sat down and immediately felt like I had entered another world.

The six African-American students, the executive board of the soon-to-be-formed choir, were eager to get their group started and were all talking at once. I watched them interact. I listened as they agreed, disagreed, and bickered about how the choir should proceed. In the midst of the bickering, one young man, the president of the group, called above the clamor, "All right, before we begin the meeting, let's pray." Dutifully, the six students joined hands—and reached for mine as well. Admittedly, I hadn't prayed since the last time my cat was at the vet, but I grabbed the outstretched hands and, for the first time, felt like part of the group.

As the weeks rolled along, we began to trust each other. I went to every meeting and advised them on how to create a constitution, procure space for their first concert, and raise money. They reciprocated by making me feel part of, even valued in, their gospel choir. I was their counsel and had found my place in the group. However, when the conversation moved to fundraising, I quickly lost my place again. The students decided on a soul food sale just before Thanksgiving. They would make all the food, arrange with Food Service to borrow chafing dishes and sterno, set up a table in the Student Center, and sell fried chicken, macaroni and cheese, collards, and sweet potato pie for $5 a plate. It was entrepreneurship at its best.

Not looking for my guidance or advice, they divided all of the cooking responsibilities, until they came to the sweet potato pie. Although apparently masters of frying and sautéing, no one seemed comfortable with baking. This is where I knew I could help. A novice cook with generally good results, I immediately blurted out to the group, "I'll make the pies!" They looked at me with grins in their hearts that were trying to bubble up to their too respectful lips.

Finally, Jamilah broke the uncomfortable moment and said, "That's OK. I'll just ask my mom." But I persisted, "No, I can do it. I'm a pretty good cook." The students smiled at each other playfully, until one of them giggled innocently and said, "You think you can make sweet potato pie?" With only a little bit of doubt in my heart, I resolutely affirmed that I was up to the task, despite their understandable doubts. Out of respect for me, and perhaps sheer desperation, they agreed to let me try my hand at their favorite soul food dessert.

I spent the next few weeks searching for recipes. I scoured *Cooking Light*, *Gourmet*, and *The Joy of Cooking* for the best recipe but soon began to doubt my resolve. Since I had never even tasted sweet potato pie, how could I tell a good recipe from a bad one? I certainly couldn't ask the students for a recipe. That would show them my insecurity. So I went to an expert, one of my colleagues at the university who was a soul food expert. After she had a good laugh, she brought me a recipe the very next day. Although I expected an old, tattered family recipe card that had been handed down for generations, she handed me a recipe cut from *Woman's Day*.

The night before the Thanksgiving soul food sale, with my heart racing and my palms sweaty, I cooked sweet potatoes, beat them, sweetened them, flavored them, tasted them, and baked them into three pies. The next morning, I proudly but anxiously delivered them to the Student Center. At lunchtime, I hesitantly walked over to the sale to see how my students were doing and to buy my lunch in support of their efforts. As soon as Jamilah saw me, she yelled across the Student Center lobby, "Hey! You kicked it!"

I looked behind me, but when I didn't see anyone there, I pointed to my chest. "Me?"

"Yeah! You kicked the pie!"

"Is that a good thing?" I asked naively.

"Yes! It tastes like my mom's. We're almost sold out!" And with that, Jamilah gave me a hug, and I knew that I had become part of something special. I had become more than red-tape-advisor. I had earned the students' trust and gained a new cultural awareness in the process. My students had learned that "administration" could be more than red tape—it could also mean support. Through that support, they learned to trust me and accept me into their gospel choir. I learned what it was like to be on the outside, not to take trust for granted, and to make sweet potato pie.

At the end of that academic year, the gospel choir gave me a gift: a clock that had my name inscribed, along with the title, "Trusted Advisor." Five years and a job change later, that clock still sits on my desk. It's a testimony and warm reminder about why I work in student affairs.

STUDENT AFFAIRS—IT'S NOT JUST A JOB!

BY

LEE E. BIRD

"It's not just a job, it's an adventure" was the promotional phrase used by the Navy some years ago to attract recruits. The same thing could be said about a career in student affairs. A quick glance at our schedule might suggest that our jobs are, well, "normal": staff meetings, committees, supervisory tasks, planning, problem solving, and a special event or two. The problem is that our lives rarely resemble what is printed in the calendar. Much of the "adventure" we face takes place after 5 p.m. and ends sometime before we go home to change for our 8 a.m. meeting. We see the good, the bad, and the ugly and somehow gather our courage to live the adventure day after day and year after year. Before we know it, we've spent 25 to 30 years collecting stories that only those in the profession can relate to or, frankly, believe.

Consider this putative letter home from one of our students:

> Dear Mom,
> I got a "B" on my last chemistry exam. My homework is piling up, but I hope to catch up real soon. Thanks for your last letter and the Top Ramen coupons. Not much is new.
>
> We had another drug bust in the hall last night. It went down really fast because the police were already here. By the way, we finally caught the yahoo that kept chucking chairs from the 8th floor window. This time he almost hit the fireman, whew! Close call! Oh yeah, the firemen were here because some idiot swung on a sprinkler head and snapped it off. He said he did it because he saw a tarantula. It turned out it wasn't a tarantula at all, just a furry piece of pizza one of the guys threw into the hallway because it smelled so bad.
>
> Do you remember the summer we all went to the falls at Yellowstone? Well, the sprinkler water looked a lot like that, gently cascading down four flights of stairs – only this water was brown and chunky. It sure was lucky this happened when it did though. They had to shut off all the water in the building to repair the sprinkler head. Just when they got the water off, we saw the smoke belching out of the kitchen. They are still trying to determine the exact cause of the fire. It seems it was either a case of spontaneous combustion due to food debris left in the oven, or twice baked brownies. They can't be sure.

Thankfully, we still had enough water in the stairwell to start a bucket brigade to put out the fire in the kitchen. No real damage was done and my hall council immediately commissioned a mural to connect the water stains to the burn marks. It looks real neat. Tell Dad I said hi. Please write again soon.

Love,
Sarah

P.S. My hall director said I should ask you if I've ever had the measles and if my tetanus shot is current.

My parents suggested that I keep a journal after calling them with wild tales about life in the halls as a hall director and administrator in residential life. I failed to start that journal, convinced that I would always remember the details of these tales from the "dark side." From campus to campus, state to state, and position to position, wild stories seemed to be the constant. While these are the stories we shared with colleagues (much like cops and ER docs), our work entails so much more. We have the opportunity to make a difference in the lives of our students each and every day by listening, caring, advising, referring, lead-ing, and serving as good role models. Some days we even create a miracle or two in the minds of the students we serve. Like the Marines, we are the few, the proud, etc. We were selected to prepare for this special duty. We are the people who dedicate our lives to making the college experience better, fuller, richer, and more meaningful for our students, sometimes against great odds. We battle alco-hol abuse, depression, drugs, violence, discrimination, fire, flood, and mayhem side by side with our students to help make them academically successful, good leaders, and good, well-rounded human beings.

Last week (May 25, 2005), we laid to rest Dr. Marcia Dickman who, in her long career, served as both a student affairs practitioner and professor of educational development. She prepared master's- and doctoral-level students for careers in student affairs. Following the funeral mass, we gathered in the Student Union at Oklahoma State University to tell her family and friends of the difference she made in so many lives both in and out of the classroom. Her abiding passion for the profession, warmth, wit, compassion for the students, and understanding of student development prepared generations of graduate students to lead and to serve the next generation. In that room, we laughed, cried, and laughed some more about her unique way of teaching and her impact on others. She will never be forgotten.

If we are really lucky and blessed, one day we will be laid to rest, and past and current students and colleagues will gather together to share stories and tell of the difference we made in their lives. Until that day comes, cherish and save those precious notes you receive each year from students and parents. While they may not seem like much at the time, they are the purest and most meaning-ful "evidence" of a life lived well in the profession.

Rest in peace, Dr. "D."

A LETTER TO JAMI – ONE WHO MADE A DIFFERENCE

BY
JANET E. WALBERT

Dear Jami,

It has been more than four years since we lost you. I often think about how much you meant to me, and then I realize it is more like how much you "mean" to me. You are still very much present in my life.

I think about my first real memory of you as a student. You were a sophomore and a very outgoing orientation leader. I was walking across our small, cozy campus and you were walking backwards, pointing, and describing our beloved college to a group of prospective students and their parents. You never missed a step as you described the physical features and the intangible qualities of our campus. Then you saw me out of the corner of your eye. You shouted, "Hi, Toots!" then said calmly to the tour group, "That's our dean of students." Of course, my response was, "Hi, Jami" with a wave, but I was thinking, "Who does she really think she is, calling me Toots?" The relationship we built on those occasions—because the scene replayed itself almost weekly—was something that was stronger than most friendships.

You always had a way of bringing a smile to my face. Your energy preceded you into a room and remained long after you left. Your artistic talents are still part of my office. I even have a Post-It note you left me—rediscovered a few months after you died—that simply says, "Love Ya Toots!"

When I think of students who have changed my life, you are always on the list. It isn't because of what I was able to do for you. It was really what we were able to do together. Your youthful wisdom, your willingness to teach me about Passover traditions, your honest response when you didn't know how to do something or how to spell a word were simple ways you touched my life and let me into yours. Watching you grow, learn, and touch the lives of others will forever be part of my favorite memories. Maybe it is the underpinning of why I do what I do.

Jami, your sudden departure from this world as we know it was devastating to many of us. But your ability to be here, to be present when you were alive, and to be with us years later is extraordinary. In your 22 years on this earth, you positively touched more lives than most people do in three or four times the number of years.

What I want to say is that I am not sure who gave or got more: you, the very special student whom I was supposed to support and nurture, or me, the dean whose life was touched, changed, and forever strengthened because you were you. You helped me laugh and let me be Toots to you. You taught me never to underestimate the possible influence I might have on someone or, more important, the possible influence someone might have on me. Thanks.

Toots

AN UNEXPECTED THANKS

BY

JAMES RHATIGAN

I write this approaching age 70, having worked with students since my first days in the residence halls at Syracuse in the 1950s. One very important lesson is etched in my mind: "Any one day, any one encounter can make a difference in our lives or the life of a student."

I do not look back on the days of high drama, awards, or recognitions. No, it is the ordinary days that produced the significant stories of my life, the days that seem indistinguishable from one another. If you want to see the power of an ordinary day, talk to someone who will never see one again.

Experienced administrators spend time on the "big picture" manifested in planning and strategic thinking. The best part of my life, though, was centered on the small picture—one student, one issue. Rarely did I have a long history with most of the students I encountered. They appeared at a point in time. Our lives converged perhaps only that one time. I learned that usually it was not the depth of our relationship that made a difference, it was the timing. In this circumstance, one either is helpful or is not. We had better work hard to make that first encounter effective. There likely will be no second chance.

I retired from full-time work in 2002 and received a note from a woman who noticed the announcement in the local paper. The woman said, "I want to thank you for the help you gave me and my son in 1971." I did not recall this woman or her son, but I was intrigued and called to thank her for writing. I asked her to remind me of the circumstances. She had been referred to me by someone in the registrar's office. She had come to the campus to withdraw her son from school because he was convicted of possessing marijuana (a felony at the time) and was going to have to spend several months in jail. When we met, I promised her that we would all work together to put her son on a better path once he finished his sentence.

The son never did require my assistance, and I never saw his mother again. Why is it that this woman would remember this incident to the extent that she would take the time to write 31 years later? It was those few words of hope, words that never were backed up in later behavior. Our meeting had an efficacy for her far greater than anything I could have imagined. It illustrates the enduring quality of a single encounter.

Student affairs has been preoccupied for much of its history by a concern for professionalism. Some administrators I know have sought professional recognition from the outside, certified by others, usually a top-down proposition. I hope that one day we come to realize that professionalism comes from the bottom up, is based on a perfect mix of competency and caring, and can neither be given to us nor taken from us.

From the first day on the job, we will see people who are in trouble, who aspire, or who want to share their excitement. What we are not likely to see on that first day is the difference the encounter may mean in lengthening time. We just have to take this on faith. If we do, we will seldom be disappointed. This is the beauty of our work and a key to understanding why it is such an exciting way to spend a lifetime.

LETTER OF RECOMMENDATION

BY

JIM D. HARDWICK

"I am not sure I would be the best person to write you a letter of recommendation" was my response to the request to serve as a reference for a graduating senior. He replied, "But you know me better than anyone else at the college." As the dean of campus life at a small liberal arts college who handled a considerable number of student conduct cases, I had to agree with him. The student had been in and out of trouble for his entire four years. I firmly believed that his ethical compass had no true north. At one point, he had used his talents with computer technology and his charm with the custodians to get into an office after hours to use the college's ID equipment to "explore" producing fake driver's licenses. At another point, I accompanied him to small claims court when the student government and the college were being sued for an oral contract he allegedly made on behalf of both groups.

"Given what I know about you, what would you want me to write in your letter of recommendation?" "The truth," he said. He told me he was applying for a computer fraud prevention position with a Fortune 500 credit card company. He thought that I had the best understanding of how he could apply his computer science skills to understanding the criminal mind. He was not sure his computer science faculty fully understood his deviant side. He wanted me to describe all of the boundary testing he had done at college as examples of how he had used his computer and creative skills to break, bend, or violate all of the rules. The student wanted the recruiter for the Fortune 500 company to understand that he knew how to anticipate fraud and a criminal mind.

His final plea was that I was one of the only people on campus who knew he had committed all of these offenses behind the scenes. There was no one else who could fully write about his deviance.

I offered to write the letter of recommendation with the understanding that I would have to be honest about his strengths and weaknesses. I told him that I would let him read the letter, and if he wanted to use it, he could. If he didn't like the letter, he was not obligated to use me as a reference for the position. I fully expected that when I was through writing his letter of recommendation, the student would choose to not have his deviance revealed to a future employer.

The student used the letter of recommendation that I wrote for him. He interviewed for the job and was hired instantly. The feedback from the recruiter was that my letter outlining his deviant side was a stroke of genius. The letter helped him sell the skills that he believed would be an asset to the company if it hired him.

Who knew getting in trouble at college would be a marketable job skill?

THE ROBE: CONFESSIONS OF A NEW FACULTY MEMBER

BY

CAROL A. LUNDBERG

After working in student affairs for about a decade, I entered a doctoral program in hopes of further advancement up the administrative ladder. While in graduate school, I realized the ladder more interesting to me was the one for faculty members. The prospect of engaging with students around papers and research lured me from a career focused on learning outside the classroom to one more focused inside the classroom. It also looked to me like that work happened between the hours of 9 and 5, not at the midnight lip sync or the weekend orientation programs, where so much of my student affairs work had seemingly occurred.

When I finished my doctoral work, one of the big questions among my graduate student colleagues scrambling for faculty positions was whether to rent or buy regalia for the commencement ceremony. After pondering the weighty questions posed in our coursework, perhaps we welcomed the seemingly mundane question of whether to rent or buy. I decided to rent, for fear that the financial investment of purchasing a robe was unwise. I did not have a job offer, and there was no guarantee that I would get one. Perhaps the Ph.D. was just a good learning experience, not actually preparation for a career as a teacher and scholar. Besides, I didn't feel like a scholar. Scholars don't change diapers, forget appointments, or burn meals, do they? I told myself I would buy the robe if I got a faculty position.

A month later, I got that faculty position but not the robe. As I was introduced to others with "Dr." in front of my name, it was hard not to chuckle. Who ever heard of a professor teaching a class with a knee-high stuck to the back of her dress via static cling? How much they didn't know about the person they called "Dr."!

As a new faculty member in a student affairs professional preparation program, I taught several courses for a cohort of 14 new graduate students. They were going to become student affairs professionals, eager to learn so that they could engage the world of students, families, faculty, and administrators. It was my task to help them develop new ideas, understand theory, master assessment practice, and more. I met them for the first day of classes in a "smart" classroom, replete with computer and projector. What I thought it lacked was a "smart" professor. In one class, I couldn't seem to add up the points on my syllabus

23

correctly, leading to a possible point total of 105, rather than 100. It didn't help that the course was Statistics. It was definitely not time to buy a robe.

Did my students realize they were getting a novice? Would they grant me some grace? I tried to teach classes in the same style that I had seen my own professors teach, but I couldn't tell if I was impersonating them well enough. Did my students look at me in the same way the kind neighbor looks at the little boy dressed up like Dracula on Halloween? She pretends to be afraid, and the little boy feels good about his Dracula costume. Were students pretending to learn just so I would feel good about my role as a new professor? The prospect of donning a robe would just verify the image of myself as the trick-or-treating professor. Perhaps this faculty role was just a temporary foray into the world of academia. I loved my work in student affairs, and I thought I could re-enter it relatively easily. Besides, that would free me from the need to purchase the robe.

I thought publication would be a good indicator that I was a "real" scholar. I would wait to buy a robe until an article was accepted for publication. Early in that first year, I learned that an article of mine was accepted, then another, and another. Time for a robe? Probably not. Those articles grew from my dissertation. I should wait to buy the robe until an article was published based on a new study using data not from my dissertation. I loved my research, my work in the classroom, and especially my students, but that didn't seem enough to make me robe-worthy. My 14 students now felt more like colleagues than students. I had cried in front of them, made errors in front of them, laughed with them, and loved them, but those activities didn't fit my own concept of what makes one a "scholarly professor." They were activities very familiar to me as a student affairs professional, but did they fit with the academic role?

Near the end of my second year of teaching, I faced the reality that the students who began their master's program in my class would be graduating soon. It was a bittersweet realization. I had grown close to those 14 students. As part of their graduation requirement, they had to demonstrate competence in 12 areas central to our field. As I attended the colloquiums during which they presented their learning and evidence of their competence, I realized they had learned. Even more shocking, I realized they had learned from me. A phrase that I had learned when I was teaching Sunday school as a college student echoed in my mind: "The teacher has not taught until the student has learned." My students had learned, so perhaps I had taught.

As I strolled back to my office after one student's excellent colloquium, I wondered about the robe. I reflected on the way my firstborn child made me a mother. Some would argue that he made me a mother when he was conceived, others when he was born, and still others would say it happened somewhere in between the two. What convinced me that I was a mother was what happened between us. He taught me how to be his mother. On hard days, I worried that he was getting a raw deal since I had to learn everything with him. Wouldn't he be better off with a more experienced mother? Perhaps I should have had a practice run first. Likewise, I was learning with my students, but wouldn't it be better if they had a teacher who had already learned? I especially worried about this for the 14 students who had me for several courses. Would they and their students be at a disadvantage down the road because I was a beginner? Then I thought about the conference presentations we had done together, the questions we had raised for one another, and the moments when I could see progress. I realized that in much the same way that my son made me a mother, my 14 students had made me a teacher, perhaps even a scholar. Together, we had learned.

I ordered the robe. No sirens or flashing lights went off when I told the bookstore clerk that I wanted to order a robe; perhaps the imposter alarm was malfunctioning that day. The clerk measured me, and I was on my way. I went to work, sat in my little office, and wondered if I had jumped the gun.

Commencement took place a month later. I felt a bit odd in my fancy robe, despite the fact that the room was full of people in fancy robes. I went to find my 14 students in the line of graduates, in their less fancy robes. After some talk about follow-up interviews from the NASPA and ACPA conferences, it was time for us to separate: faculty in one line, students in another. I would have much preferred their line; the role of student was familiar to me, as were the 14 people I had grown to love in that line. Many times in my student affairs days, I had told parents at orientation that it was time for them to leave their children and go home. In much the same way that I had told parents to go home, the announcer told faculty and students that it was time to separate. After 14 hugs, my students joked with me that they liked my robe better than theirs and asked where they could get one. I explained it would take a little more schooling, a few more papers, but that they could all do it. As I wiped a tear from my cheek, I told them that in addition to all of that, it might also take a partnership with 14 students.

LIFELINES

BY

MELINDA MANNING

Contestants on the game show *Who Wants to be a Millionaire?* choose from several "lifelines" who can be called during the show to help the contestant answer any of the questions. My lifelines never helped me win a million dollars but served a far greater purpose. At times, they were the very forces that kept me on this earth. My lifelines are four largely uncelebrated individuals who never knew how many times they saved me from drowning in my own darkness.

It all began my sophomore year of college. As with many students, this was a time of change for me. I took on leadership roles, made new friends, and learned a great deal, mostly outside the classroom. It was also the year that I was raped. Like many rape survivors, I never reported the assault and didn't seek help for many years. I began to spiral downward into what I now call the "seven years of darkness." I contemplated suicide nearly every day. I plotted ways that I could kill myself and make it look like an accident. I wrote a number of wills and funeral details. Almost every morning, I prayed to have the strength to carry out my plans. At night, I cursed myself for still being alive.

Despite my own pain, I agreed to serve as co-chair of our campus rape-awareness organization. Our new advisor was a young professional in the housing department. We were pretty skeptical at first about having a male advisor, but "Jim" quickly won us over. He met with our leadership team weekly and provided much-needed guidance for our fledging organization. I started to realize how much I looked forward to those weekly meetings because of all the support and praise he provided. Those meetings were the one place I felt like my old self, and Jim was one of the few men that I felt safe being around. Looking back, I think those weekly advising meetings probably were the one thing that kept me from trying to take my life that year.

My next lifeline was "Susan," the assistant dean of students. She became my biggest cheerleader and believed in me during a time when I certainly didn't believe in myself. She inspired me to work on behalf of other sexual assault survivors. Her door was always open, and she would interrupt other work so we could talk. She helped me feel my own power again. Even though I was still haunted by my demons, their calls became easier to ignore.

After several years teaching in another part of the country, I returned to my alma mater to go to law school. Susan suggested that I apply for a position with the housing department in order to help pay for school. While serving in that position, I met lifeline number three, "David." He was my supervisor during my first year working in the department. With David's support, my housing job became a welcome respite from the harsh environment of law school. He challenged me to think about my future and what I really wanted out of life. These were questions that I had never thought about, due to my depression. I never really thought I had choices. Thanks to David, I began to seriously consider a career in student affairs.

Finally, there was "Wayne." The rigors of law school brought back much of the darkness that I had struggled with before. I didn't feel like I belonged and was convinced that I was going to fail. But Wayne was the one staff member at the law school who could make me feel like I was smart enough to be there. I accepted a job as his research assistant in order to explore options in student affairs. I'm not sure if I actually did any research, but what I gained from my time with him was tremendous. During our almost daily chats, he helped me to realize that there was no shame in going to see a therapist. As a result, I finally got help. By sharing stories about his own law school mishaps, he made me realize that it was OK if I never made the dean's list. I still could be a successful attorney—or anything else for that matter.

Here I am, writing this in my own office at the university. I just had a crying student leave, and I expect another in 30 minutes. Here I am, 13 years after my sophomore year and 13 years stronger. I am now the one dispensing the tissues, along with advice and support. Maybe I am someone else's lifeline. I don't have to call on my lifelines very often, but I think of them almost every day. I know that I owe them a debt that can never be repaid.

THE TRIUMPH OF KINDNESS AND CARING

BY
GAIL SHORT HANSON

On September 11, 2001, the president's cabinet at American University gathered in a conference room for our weekly meeting. It was the kind of fall day in Washington, D.C., when you regretted being indoors. The sun was already bright in a clear blue sky, and the temperature was still comfortably warm.

The usual small talk and banter of familiar colleagues filled the time as cabinet members entered the room. After we assembled, but before the president began the meeting, an office assistant leaned in to tell us that a plane had crashed into the World Trade Center in New York. We reacted in stunned silence, but our silence quickly gave way to speculation. Pilot error, equipment malfunction, traffic control error—nothing made sense.

Saddened, but not particularly distracted, we turned our attention to the agenda, until the conference room door opened again. This time the office assistant handed the president a note. A second plane had hit the World Trade Center. The response was not silence this time but palpable shock. How could this be possible? We turned on the television and were swept immediately into the chaos as reporters tried to make sense of it all. Each of us watched, hypnotized by unbelievable images.

The explosion of the second plane ended our speculation. This looked like a terrorist attack. Many members of our university community had family and friends in New York, and so the first moves by student services staff were aimed at mobilizing the resources to aid and comfort those whose losses from this disaster might be personal. This singular focus was almost immediately splintered by the announcements that a plane had hit the Pentagon, just miles from our campus, and that other hijacked planes might be en route to Washington. Now our concern was not solely to help our community manage its grief but to protect it from harm—perhaps from catastrophe. The Pentagon crash put everyone in motion.

The swirl of activity that ensued is difficult to recount. Everyone assumed an essential set of responsibilities based on their presence of mind and resources. Communication networks were established to control rumors and channel timely, accurate information to the university community. Counselors and chaplains were assigned to each of the residence halls and deployed at large to work with those overwhelmed by what they saw. Plans were made to add security throughout the campus and around its perimeter.

Interrupting the frenzy of purposeful activity was a call from the university chaplain to gather at noon in front of the interfaith chapel for prayer, reflection, and consolation. Gravitating to the chapel in times of distress and sadness is almost instinctive at a Methodist-affiliated institution with a strong interfaith tradition. Even before noon, small clusters of stunned people began to form on the chapel lawn, talking quietly, wiping away tears, hugging each other for comfort, staring bewilderedly at the cloudless blue sky, and awaiting speakers who might help to explain the inexplicable.

What lingers in my memory about the chapel gathering is the emotional and physical experience more than the comforting words or requests for understanding, tolerance, and forgiveness. What lingers is the feeling of an aching chest—as if in response to a sharp kick—stinging eyes, a throat constricted and choking back tears, a mind racing through a relief plan, eyes sweeping back and forth across the assembly looking for those who might need immediate support. Pride, an emotion also felt, was at odds with the others. Through our presence at the chapel and through the words spoken by our campus and faith leaders, it was clear that our community would find good in the midst of destruction. We would seek a deeper understanding of a faith whose teachings would be maligned and misunderstood in the days and weeks ahead. Perhaps most important, we would embrace and protect our Muslim brothers and sisters against the anger ignited by the terrorists' unprovoked aggression. The chapel gathering set the tone for how we would respond to the extended aftermath of the 9/11 attacks.

One of the chapel speakers asked us to take stock of our inner resources—to ask for help if we needed it, to offer help if we had it within us to give. The chaplains and counseling center staff inspired us with their presence, comforting many by simply listening to them or by being with them in silence. The community service center quickly became the hub for volunteer activities. Students were already walking to the Pentagon, hoping to join rescue efforts there. Others wanted to organize a blood drive or travel to donor centers. Many in student services extended themselves to students and colleagues as the need for aid and support stretched from early morning to late into the night.

Communication with students' families was a constant. Understandably, frightened parents wanted assurances that their sons and daughters were safe on campus, that the university's safety precautions were thorough, that we had an emergency plan, that we would communicate any new developments, and that students distressed by the attacks would be afforded some leniency in completing assignments and taking examinations.

As the next two days unfolded, we learned that, miraculously, not one community member had lost an immediate family member in the attacks. It was the sheer trauma of the incidents and their televised repetitions that took their toll, diverting us from studies and routine activities and robbing us of rest. Fighter jets circled over the capital city, keeping vigil against another attack. Their droning engines distracted us, interrupted our sleep, and triggered disturbing dreams.

By Thursday, September 13, some sense of normalcy was seeping back into campus life. Then a telephone call to the front desk of our largest residence hall shattered the fragile calm. The caller said there was a bomb on campus.
Within minutes, the news was conveyed to the public safety office and campus officials. Local and federal law enforcement officers converged on the campus with dogs and ordered a full-scale evacuation. Evacuation of 84 acres and 37 campus buildings, early on a weekday morning—it had never been done. There were no protocols.

Fire alarms were pulled in all the residence halls and classroom and office buildings. As people poured out, staff stood near the entrances informing them that we had received a bomb threat. Students leaving their residence halls were in a daze, shaken from sleep by clanging alarms and resident staff banging on doors. Many were in various states of undress, some without shoes, as they assumed that a hall evacuation was a false alarm and that they soon would be back in their beds. This morning was an exception. Everyone was directed to a large, open, off-campus parking lot across the street from the main quadrangle.

As was the case on 9/11, the evacuation and events of the day took shape like an improvised play. Without assigned or rehearsed roles, members of the campus community took up posts directing people and traffic on the busy streets surrounding the campus. Some determined the availability of nearby churches and small shopping malls to shelter evacuees who had nowhere else to go and were inadequately dressed to stay outside for long. Over the course of the day, telephone calls to other campuses in town produced sweat suits, socks, and shoes from bookstores and water and sandwiches from food services. Supplies found their way to us slowly because of disruptions throughout the city caused by hastily established security checkpoints, road closings, and detours; locked-down government buildings; erratic public transportation; and closed airports.

Students with apartments near campus took people home with them; some with access to their cars left the area or volunteered to help transport others. They traded an uncertain future in an open parking lot for uncertainty on the roads, spending hours in traffic snarls. Many could not reach their cars because the main campus parking garage was located at the center of the sealed-off campus.

As the day wore on, we learned the consequences of hurried departures from rooms and offices: parents unable to retrieve children in daycare; people with medical conditions aggravated by missed doses of medication or skipped meals; nearly everyone prevented from meeting some particular obligation because of what they had left behind on campus or because they had no means to leave the evacuation site—no car keys, no identification, no credit cards, no money. Most cell phone service was down. Student services staff and others circulated through the crowd, inquiring about people's needs and sharing what information there was about when we might be permitted to return to campus, when food and water might be available, how transportation might be arranged to the nearest hospital. Some discovered a bit of genius for problem-solving. Students with operating cell phones became calling centers, lending their phones to others to call their worried families. A quick negotiation with a neighborhood coffee shop yielded bathroom privileges for evacuees. Periodically, we gave thanks that it was a beautiful day with moderate temperatures. It was possible for people to wait outdoors for hours without suffering from the weather.

How long does it take to search 84 acres and 37 buildings for a bomb? We now know the answer: about six hours. A few brave volunteers walked through their buildings after being briefed on what constitutes a "suspicious package." The security professionals and their dogs did most of the work. Late in the afternoon, the public safety office announced that the campus was clean. No bomb was found. We could return to our buildings and our activities. Those who remained stranded in the parking lot slowly dispersed.

With the reopening of the campus, there were new challenges to confront. Most dining services and housekeeping personnel had gone home. There were few people to perform essential services. In addition to renewing efforts to calm students and respond to their parents, many student services staff and student leaders stepped forward to work in the cafeteria and to help clean the residence halls until regular support staff returned.

Two days after the bomb scare, classes resumed and a second level of activity began to take shape. Many senior student services staff connected with faculty colleagues to plan teach-ins on Islam, the history and politics of the Middle East, the psychology of terrorism, and related topics. The staff of International Student Services made extraordinary efforts to reach the several hundred students from the Middle East. Their interventions were complex. Some of these students were afraid to leave their homes. A few were accosted as they moved through communities beyond the campus. A number of international students were summoned back to their countries by their governments or their families. The implications of these premature departures for students' immigration statuses and academic programs occupied advisors as they worked to ensure that the students made the best possible decisions about their futures.

Communication with students' families continued to consume the senior student services staff, even as the president and the university relations office labored to post regular updates on the university's Web site to assure families that life on campus was slowly returning to a familiar routine. It is difficult to say when routine was restored. But at some point, more than a week after the 9/11 attacks, we seemed to turn a corner. People were still terribly tired and not sleeping well, but we were no longer waiting for the next crisis.

It was just on the leading edge of this turnaround that a letter from the university president was delivered to the Office of Student Services. It is not too much to say that it transformed student services' sense of its place in the university community. Here is the president's letter, dated September 19, 2001:

Office of Student Services Staff
American University
Washington, DC 20016

Dear Student Services Staff:

The tidal wave of events that crashed in upon us last week was devastating enough to have left us disabled and disoriented as an institution and a community. That it did not is due in great measure to the heroic efforts you undertook immediately and for "24-7" support day after day after day.

It is not just that you were there when students, faculty, and other staff needed someone like you to be there, you were there communicating a deep sense of caring, of calm, of support, of expertise. You knew what to do and how to do it, and you kept doing it well beyond what might have been expected.

I understand as only a few others can that the reason you were so accomplished in this moment of crisis is because of what you deal with every day all year long. You would not, could not, be in Student Services if at some point in your life you had not already decided that you care a great deal about people and that you want to spend your time finding ways to assure that they are healthy and whole, and that they grow. I want you to know that that decision and the ways you have fulfilled it at AU at a time when we desperately needed it has helped turn an undeniably tragic event into something we will always remember as a moment of the triumph of kindness and caring because of your leadership.

At AU we can never speak of education again without including what and how you taught us. From the bottom of my heart and on behalf of all your colleagues and students, thank you!

With pride and gratitude,

Benjamin Ladner
President

THERE IS A LESSON IN FOOTBALL

BY

ROBERT E. DIXON

It has been difficult to find the lessons in my father's teachings. The wisdom was not always transparent, and after his death, nearly a quarter of a century ago, I continue to discover his quiet influence on my life.

My father received no formal education past high school, but he was intelligent. He lacked sophistication, but he was far from ignorant. He loved his family and cared deeply for people, but he was not affectionate. He was a good man, but he was a hard man. My father was complex in an ordinary way, and the lessons he taught usually took years to understand.

One such lesson has taken me some 30 years to fully grasp, but I vividly remember that the lesson began in the fall of 1973. My father and I were given tickets to a Georgia Tech football game. I had never been to a college game, and my dad took the tickets under the pretext of "going for Bobby's sake."

It was a Saturday, early in October, when my father and I headed north to Atlanta and the game. I was excited, and if my father was excited, he hid it extremely well. It was nearly a three-hour drive, and we left shortly before 6 a.m. for a game that started at 1 p.m. I'm sure my questions flowed like a river during most of the trip. There is little worse than a 13 year old with an array of questions posed to an adult with few answers.

I think we were at the halfway point of the trip when he finally told me to "hush." "Hush" was a code word in my family. "Hush" said, "Be quiet," in the harshest tone possible. If the phrase "shut up" was ever used, the house emptied because it meant someone, usually the one in arm's reach, would be in harm's way.

Several minutes passed, and I could no longer contain myself. "Dad, why are we getting there so early?"

"Son, today is Georgia Tech's homecoming, and I thought we would get there in time to walk around the campus and see a few things before the game." He spoke in a quiet tone. He seemed a bit too melancholy, too reflective for the man I'd always known as one whose only expressed emotions were anger and frustration.

"Huh?" I replied like a kid who thought the football stadium was the only building on campus.

"Damn it, Bobby." He often used this phrase while addressing me. It was used so much that my mother thought I might eventually sign my school papers as damn it Bobby. Pavlov's dog, and Pavlov himself, could have learned from me. I usually jumped quickly when I heard "damn it, Bobby."

"There are more things at Georgia Tech than football." His tone was condescending. I knew it well.

"Name one," I demanded of the sage driving the car. If his voice could interject such an all-knowing attitude, I was going to make him back it up.

"Damn it, Bobby. Hush. There are plenty." He was clearly becoming agitated.

"Name one." I kept it up as if I was pushing the old man into a wager.

"Alexander Memorial Coliseum. You know, the basketball building."

"Georgia Tech doesn't have a basketball team." This was prior to the Bobby Cremins era when Georgia Tech became a basketball powerhouse.

"Yes, they do. Not much of one, but they do."

"So what else, huh?" I pushed a little too hard.

"Just shut up." His voice was starched.

"So what else?" The feeling that I had gone too far swept across me like a cold wind. I had crossed the line. I had forgotten the code, and I saw his hand begin to twitch on the steering wheel. "Oh, my God," I thought. "I am going to die. He'll toss my body beside the interstate and tell mama I was kidnapped in Atlanta. The State Patrol would eventually find my bruised and mangled body. The cause of death would be eventually ruled a justifiable homicide. 'He wouldn't hush,' my dad would calmly explain to the police. My grave would be etched, 'Damn it, Bobby. He finally shut up.' The crime would never go to trial, because the jury would surely acquit my dad. The other fathers on the jury would completely understand that the crime was justified, because they had their own 'Damn it, Bobbys' at home."

I cringed, expecting to feel my head bounce off the dashboard, but nothing happened. There were no broken bones, and there was no blood. In my utter fear, I heard him quietly say, "I've never been on a big college campus before, and I want to look around. I've not had many chances like this."

35

I was simply glad my head was still attached to my body. I cared very little about anything else for those next few moments. Then the excitement set in again. I was going to see Georgia Tech play—live and in person. I loved Georgia Tech football.

In 1973, ESPN didn't exist, and the NCAA regulated which teams were televised. Georgia Tech rarely made the cut for broadcast, but I listened intently to the play-by-play on the Georgia Tech Radio Network. I remembered hearing big plays by great players against the great teams like Auburn, Georgia, Tennessee, and Notre Dame. The radio voices always painted the perfect picture of football. My heartbeat seemed to be controlled by the man behind the microphone. I made many tackles and scored many make-believe touchdowns on my living room floor while listening to the broadcasts.

As we neared the Georgia Tech campus, I looked across the interstate and saw the transom lights of Grant Field. Today, Grant Field (Bobby Dodd Stadium) is the oldest on-campus football stadium in the United States. This is the same field where John Heisman (namesake of the Heisman Trophy) walked the sidelines, and scores of All-Americans, as well as those lesser known, became legends.

We parked and began our walk toward the Tech campus, down North Avenue passed The Varsity. Billed as the world's largest and oldest drive-in, the Varsity has possibly the greasiest and best hamburgers, hot dogs, and chili ever created. The smell of fried onion rings rolled onto the street like a fog in a horror movie. The food is tasty, and nearly everyone within a mile of Grant Field on game day will have eaten at The Varsity before the day is over.

I guess the fried onion smell had gotten to Dad. It was 10 in the morning, and the man was going to get a chili dog and onion rings. One thing I knew from travels with my dad was when he decided to eat, you better be ready as well. It would be a long time before he got the urge again.

The Varsity is part of the culture of Georgia Tech. It is as much a part of the curriculum as calculus. The Varsity is part of game day. The sights, the sounds, the smells, and the colors of college football are created in places like The Varsity in every college town in America, and we experienced The Varsity tradition as we stood in line with those dressed in the gold and white of Tech pride.

We finished our dogs and headed on over to the campus. We continued along North Avenue, past the stadium, and into the heart of the campus. We walked through the trees scattered around the campus, and suddenly it seemed as though we were not in Atlanta anymore. I felt as though I had entered a mythical place. Old buildings stood in regal silence. I guess it hit my dad, too. He stood quietly, with an open-mouthed stare for what seemed to be an eternity. Then he said, "This is beautiful." I didn't see the beauty that he saw, but I did sense the awe. I sensed something meaningful and important, and it had nothing to do with football.

Uncharacteristic of my father, he took my hand. The oddity of a man holding his 13-year-old son's hand was quite apparent, but my dad was lost in a world that he desperately wanted me to experience with him. I didn't pull away. In the shadows of Grant Field, my dad found a place that provided meaning.

As we walked past the decorated fraternity houses, we watched generations of families and reacquainted friends gather and eat picnic lunches of fried chicken, potato salad, chips, and sandwiches while waiting for the big game.

We found the library and walked inside. How anyone could study this close to kick-off was beyond my naïve comprehension, but students huddled over tables with papers and books, pencils and protractors. We left the library and continued our walk and saw building after building lining the streets of the campus. When my dad found a building with an open door, he could not contain himself. We ventured inside. We walked down the corridors, past offices and classrooms. When rooms, offices, or labs were open, my dad found it necessary to stick his head inside.

No campus visit would be complete without stopping by the bookstore. My dad bought me a railroad engineer's hat. This was a tradition in 1973. Tech students were going to be engineers, and engineers wore the engineer's hat. I liked it. My dad bought himself a cheap pen with the Tech emblem on the side. It was gold with a black "GT" stenciled on the side. It was ugly, but he took great joy in clipping it into his shirt pocket.

Time slipped by, and we headed toward the stadium. We walked in and found our section. As we passed through the gate toward the stands, I felt the magic of college football. It was my turn to stand with my mouth open. I saw a huge stadium with a field greener than I could ever have imagined.

The stands filled slowly with fans wearing the team colors. Our seats were 10 rows behind the visitor's bench and next to the legendary Tech student body cheering section. The students were loud, obnoxious, disrespectful, and loyal to their cause. They loved their team, and they loved their school.

Duke University, the Georgia Tech opponent, entered the field first, only to be welcomed by a decidedly hostile crowd. Then the stands fell eerily quiet as the announcer introduced Tech's starting defensive team. Each starter received cheers as he entered the stadium. When the last defensive starter was announced, the screams and cheers became deafening as a gold-and-white 1930 Ford jalopy rolled out of the tunnel and split the band lining the field. The cheerleaders were hanging onto the car as it led the remaining players onto the field. The band played Rambling Wreck, and the hair stood up on the back of my neck. I looked at my dad. He was smiling. The consuming emotion of college football had taken hold of him, just as it had me. We were experiencing this thing called college football together. All was right with the world.

A few hours later, the game drew to an end, and the happy fans left the stadium. My dad and I stayed for a few extra minutes, savoring the moment. With the stands empty, my dad said this was a great day. It was a great day.

As we walked toward the North Avenue gate, he stopped, grabbed my hand, and pulled me into an alcove away from the people exiting the stadium. He turned and looked onto an empty field, straightened his back from his usual stooped posture, and took a deep breath. To this day I don't know what he was thinking, but I'll bet that he was being nostalgic for things that never happened for him and dreaming of the things waiting for me.

A few years later, my father passed away. He never experienced college football on the Georgia Tech campus—or any other campus—again. When I went through his desk shortly after his death, I found a gold pen with a gaudy black emblem worn and faded. A few sheets of notebook paper with budgets and income tax information were in the same drawer, with a few doodles featuring the letters GT inked along the margins.

My father, who never attended college, scribbled the Georgia Tech emblem during the private times of his life. My mother told me years later how desperately my dad wanted me to go to Tech. Fate, however, took me in another direction, and I have no regrets. Yet that one day on the Georgia Tech campus, for me, grew over the years into something much bigger than Tech. It created an enduring love for higher education and all things collegiate, including football.

My dad had fallen in love with Georgia Tech that fall afternoon, and he nursed a fond admiration as well as a quiet envy of Tech graduates. Through a single athletic event, he became part of Georgia Tech and its mission that was so much larger than football and the Saturday afternoons in the fall.

In the summer of 1993, I returned to Georgia Tech not to go to a football game, but to trace the other footsteps that my dad and I took two decades before. With my son and daughter in tow, we saw academic and administration buildings. We visited the stadium. With its gates open and inviting, I took Robert and Caitlin inside. We saw the section where my father and I sat that Saturday afternoon long ago, and I heard the ghosts of the game. The cheers, the heroes, and the marching band sounds were vivid memories.

In 2003, I sat in a stadium seat in tiny Stillwater, Okla., as I do on most Saturdays in autumn. This day, I was watching Oklahoma State and Kansas State play a game that meant little to the rest of the world. For the moment, though, it meant everything to the 50,000 people seated around me. Next to me sat my grown son, and for three hours on a fall afternoon we completely agreed with one another. We wanted to see Oklahoma State University excel. I did wonder, however, if anyone in the stadium that day would begin learning the lesson that football has continued to teach me for these past 30 years.

THE JOY OF E-MAIL

BY

KEN LYNDY

My wife and I both work for the student life department at a small private college. She is in charge of service learning and new-student orientation, and I am the director of Student Activities. We also codirect a peer educational theater group. The group uses drama to educate others about social issues students face in college. Topics include alcohol, peer pressure, adjustment issues, and sexual and health issues. During our rehearsals, we try to educate our student actors so they can then educate audience members after each performance.

We are constantly coordinating programs, performances, and training sessions for students, resident assistants, and other members of the campus community. Through our work with peer educators, our college became affiliated with the Bacchus and Gamma Peer Education Network, an international organization focusing on alcohol abuse prevention and related student health and safety issues. One key issue is sexual health. Such organizations often provide materials and promotional items to help with programming. One item Bacchus and Gamma made available was an educational CD-ROM about safe, practical sexual decision-making. The title of the CD is *Sex in the CD*, which is a play on the title of the hit HBO show *Sex in the City*. We thought this information would be educational, and that we could use it during some of our performances.

My wife decided to order this CD. It was to be used for housing staff training, hall programs, other off campus presentations. The CD was a "choose your own adventure" when it came to making decisions about sex. It was filled with facts and personal stories about other students' decisions. She ordered the CD and used my e-mail and shipping address because they matched up with the information on the school purchasing card.

Several weeks later, to my surprise, I received an e-mail from a business I did not recognize. The subject said, "Order confirmed and shipped." So I opened the message and the body read, "This e-mail is to confirm your order of Sex in the CD. It should arrive by Friday…" I knew this message was for my wife, so I quickly moved the mouse to the "forward message to" column of my e-mail program, the area where the address book is accessible. I quickly highlighted my wife's name, as I had numerous times in the past, and hit send. Now she would know that her CD would arrive in the mail shortly.

Well, so did every other employee on campus. Apparently, I highlighted the name under my wife's and the message was sent out to all employees on campus. I hadn't changed the message, so within minutes of sending it, I received several replies with comments like, "Was that supposed to go to all of us?" and, "That sounds like a private e-mail to me."

With a red face and some nervous laughter, I purposefully sent out another all-employee e-mail explaining what the CD was and how it would be used. The responses to that message were, "Oh, sure" and, "Yeah, right."

Since that day, I have changed some of the names on my recipient list and now move a lot slower when forwarding messages to someone.

STOCK OPTIONS

BY

TROY GILBERT

When the dot-com era was in full swing, I made my home at Stanford University, where I worked as a student affairs officer for 10 years. In those days, it was not unusual for the residence halls to be covered with flyers from local start-ups, imploring undergraduates to "...join our team...why wait until you graduate...begin those stock options right now!" Each day seemed to bring another resignation. Colleagues took jobs they claimed would double their salary.

After a couple of years, this began to affect me. My close friend and fellow staff member, Peter, after learning about yet another Stanford defection, turned to me and said with resignation, "Boy, that train is leaving and we sure ain't on it." Even on weekends, friends would push me to "...find a real job in the business world...you are so talented...use it to make some money...you'll never get rich quick by working for a university!" Heck, I wouldn't even get rich slow by working for a university.

It seemed at the time that the key to future financial success was stock options—and in student affairs we sure didn't have them. After 15 years in the field, it seemed to me that perhaps I already had had plenty of "positive student impact." I had helped lots of students, and I had gone as far in higher education as I was probably going to go. I became fascinated with what work would be like in the business world. So I left.

The transition wasn't difficult. I landed a job recruiting for a ubiquitous clothing retail giant headquartered in San Francisco, so I didn't have to move. Thanks to the clothing discounts, my wardrobe improved. It wasn't a dot-com, but it was adjusting all of its business practices to "the new economy." Thanks to the fast-paced business environment, my work efficiency improved. Thanks to a work environment completely alien to anything I had ever experienced, I learned more about myself in a scant two years than I had learned the previous 10.

My days in the corporate world were filled with the stinging urgency of filling positions. I was a researcher for the recruiting department. When a managerial or executive position opened, I researched people in the field who had the necessary talents. I would call them, get them interested, and turn over the résumés to a senior recruiter who interviewed them and sealed the deal.

The product lines, the fast-moving business organization, and the smart people with whom I worked were energizing.

One day, though, I reached a turning point. I received accolades on some work I did, some very hard work—some "stay up late, feel the pressure, live with it morning/noon/night, re-do the spreadsheets again, talk to more people" kind of hard work. I should have felt rewarded for a job well done. But I felt empty. The heart and soul I had put into the job helped to hire more financial analysts. These people would help the company better understand where the money was going so they could identify cuts, so the company could be more profitable. I felt hollow. I hadn't really helped anyone—we all got bonuses at the end of the year if the company did well. If the stock rose, so did our options. That was all the good I had done.

You know, even on your worst day in student affairs, you can have a "teachable moment" with a student that he or she (or you) could remember for the rest of your lives. Nothing in the corporate world ever had that dimension.
I was surprised. Surprised by how much I needed to work in a context of learning. What did I ultimately want my life to be about? While in the corporate world, I didn't spend sleepless nights thinking about new ways to hire good people or new approaches to retail denim. I spent sleepless nights thinking about what elements of the corporate organizational structure and project management delivery systems would have benefited students the most back in the Office of Student Activities. I spent many sleepless nights remembering those miraculous moments when a student group had done a truly great thing and how I had a renewed sense of hope in the world because of them. I didn't care about clothing retail the way I cared about student development work.

Thus, the moral of my little tale of stock options—they can have them. I am content with my small retirement account. I am content with it because of the inestimable emotional wealth I have after being part of so many key student educational experiences, experiences that can make a lasting mark on future leaders. I am content with the slowness and bureaucracy of the educational institution because the educational enterprise—the research mission, the teaching mission, the service—is such a gift to our society. I love everything about the university. I love the challenges of working with faculty. I love hearing about new research breakthroughs. I love my interaction with colleagues. I love the energy brought to our department by new professionals from other institutions.

After two long years, I left the corporate world. I now have a magnificent job developing programs to meet the academic support needs of first-year students. I have pictures in my office of student living groups that I have advised and supported. I have interesting conversations with people every day about the educational enterprise and how we can improve it.

At a recent cocktail party full of corporate people, a friend invited a few others to join our conversation. "Come over here," she beckoned them, and introduced me. "He works at UC Berkeley and he has the most interesting job." I concur. No stock options. But I am wealthy.

TWO SIDES OF A BOX OF KLEENEX

BY

KRIS OLDS

Student conduct during the first week of the semester is a special type of joy. The violations tend to be related to the gathering of 200-plus 18- to 22-year-olds, many away from home for the first time. This newfound independence can be exhilarating for the students and make for long days—and nights—for student affairs professionals.

At the beginning of my fourth year as a hall director, I thought I had it all under control. I had my system, which basically consisted of meeting with policy violators, hearing their side of the story, and deciding on an appropriate sanction. Both my personal philosophy and our departmental philosophy called for educational sanctions. Coming up with an educational sanction for a student who threw ice cream cones at his neighbor's window can sometimes be a challenge, but I always search for the "teachable moment." Sometimes I find it, other times students go through the motions.

One day in early September, I was reading incident reports and arranging conduct meetings. I came across an incident report detailing four young men smoking marijuana in a room. Two of the students were upperclassmen. I was familiar with them, and they were familiar with our conduct system. I sighed and scheduled their meetings for the next week, resolving that this would be the time that I got through to them and would see a change in their behavior. The other two were first-year students. Scheduling their meetings for the following week, I closed the conduct binder with thoughts of how to reach these two students who had started their college career smoking pot.

A week later, the conduct meeting with the returning residents was over. I gave them my patented "Choices Speech," which basically says that people have choices and choices have consequences. My role as a hall director was to help residents make choices that would help them achieve their goals. When they made choices that were in violation of our policies, I would encourage them, as adults, to take responsibility for those choices. I also would toss in some words about future repercussions if the same choices were made again. Typically, my speech is effective and contributes to the development of our students into responsible adults.

When I met with one of the new students involved in the marijuana incident, I found a very smooth-talking freshman who had obviously wormed himself out of other situations with his charm and a smile. We had a pleasant conversation about his early transition to college and the joys of being away from home for the first time. When I brought up the reason for our meeting, he gave me a 1,000-watt grin and said, "C'mon, Kris. What harm were we doing? It was just a little pot on a Friday night." I smiled back and asked how his classes were going. The grin dimmed a little.

"Well, they're a lot harder than high school classes were, but I'm sure I'll manage," he responded.

I saw my point of entry. "I imagine they are. I know students sometimes take advantage of the flexibility of an instructor's attendance policy. Have you been going to all your classes?"

He squirmed a bit in his chair, "Well, my 8 a.m. class is a bit tough to get up for. But other than that, yeah…I'm doing well."

I continued, "Have any tests or quizzes yet?"

More squirming, "Yeah…one on Friday. I think I did OK. But there were a lot of terms I had to identify, and my memory isn't too great."

Aha! Perfect transition opportunity.

"Did you know that marijuana can affect your memory? Or that it can cause sluggishness and lethargy?"

As he processed the term "lethargy," I continued. "I think an appropriate sanction would be for you to write a three-page paper on the physical and mental effects of marijuana. I want you to include examples and applications of how college students may be particularly affected."

I went on to explain our probation policy and that he needed to be on his best behavior for the next two months. I thanked him for his honesty and cooperation and let him know if he had any questions, he should feel free to stop by. He thanked me and left. I returned to my work, proud of finding "that moment" and looking forward to meeting with his roommate in the afternoon.

A few hours later, I heard a timid knock on my door. Checking the time, I prepared for the next roommate. I called for him to enter, and the door swung open. Carrying himself with none of the arrogance of his roommate, a tall, shy student stepped into my office. He glanced around, unsure of himself.

I stood, introduced myself, and asked him to sit in the wing-backed chair across from my desk. He took a seat, and I pulled out the conduct file.

"So, Mike, how are you enjoying college so far?"

He shifted a bit. "Um…it's OK."

Wanting to put him at ease, I began asking him more questions about himself. As we talked, he became more comfortable. When I was pretty sure he didn't think of me as a judge and jury, I introduced the violations, the reason for our meeting.

He looked down, and I saw tears brimming in his eyes. Now, I'm totally familiar with alligator tears and students who produce them with the intention of warming my perceived cold heart. I have to admit I was surprised to see them in the eyes of this young man. I subtly moved the box of Kleenex toward him and waited for him to speak.

He took one of the tissues, wadding it up in his hand, not making a move to wipe the one tear that was sliding down his cheek. I watched him, waiting for him to speak.

He took a deep breath and gathered himself a bit. "Kris, I'm really sorry about that. That's not the type of person I am, and I don't want people to think I'm like that."

My instant response was to reassure him that neither the staff nor I made a practice of classifying residents as "good" or "bad." But I could see he had more to say so I sat quietly, allowing him to continue his thought.

"It's just that…well…I've found it harder to meet people and make friends than I thought it would be. When those guys stopped by and asked if we wanted to hang out, I was so eager to get out of my room that I just did it. I didn't really think about what was happening. I'm not a drug user. I mean, I tried pot once in high school, but it just made me stupid. So, I just want to say that this won't happen again, and I'm very sorry."

After saying what he had to say, he slumped back in the chair, his body language indicating that he was prepared to be yelled at.

I nodded and collected my thoughts. "Well, Mike, I appreciate your honesty. I want to reassure you that the staff and I do not label students. So if your concern is that we're going to think you're a bad person, please know that that isn't going to happen." Usually, this is where the Choices Speech would come in, but

I decided against it, feeling that would only amplify his guilt. Instead, I asked about his interests. Was he an athlete? Did he enjoy politics? Was he interested in Greek life? I mentioned that there were many organizations on campus that he might be interested in and that they might offer him a chance to meet new people. He told me that he had seen a sign for an informational meeting for men's lacrosse and that he was thinking about attending. My idea for a sanction was forming.

"Mike, it's clear to me that this was a one-time thing. I think what I'd like to see you do is to find an organization or team to get involved with. I want you to meet with me in a month and tell me what you've learned and who you've made connections with. I'm also putting you on probation for two months." I explained how probation worked and that any violations that occurred during that time would imply that he was being intentional about breaking the rules and how that changed a conduct situation considerably for me. I went on to say that I wanted to see him succeed in college and to please ask me if there was anything I could do to assist with that.

He relaxed a bit. "Thanks, Kris. You won't see me here again."

I smiled. "Mike, I would love it if you would stop by on occasion and let me know how things are going. I'm not here only for students who break policy. I'm here to help students. In fact, it's the coolest part of my job."

He seemed much more at ease and, as he left, he thanked me again. I finally got to see him smile.

"This is why I do my job," I thought.

A few weeks later, one of the hall governors resigned. His academics were proving to be more challenging than he had anticipated, and he had to make some tough choices about where he was spending his time. I sent an e-mail to the other government members and to the staff, asking them to think of residents who might fill the position.

One name that popped into my head was Mike's. He had made an appointment the next day to meet with me for the follow-up to his sanction. I stuck a Post-It on his conduct file, reminding me to ask him if he'd be interested.

I was in my office the next afternoon when I heard a solid knock on my door. I called for the person to enter. In walked a confident, smiling young man. Mike had taken me up on my offer to chat on occasion, and I had watched him grow during the month. Today, he seemed even more content than usual. He dropped his bag and flopped into the chair that had once caused him so much anxiety.

"Yo, Kris. How are you doing?"

"Pretty well, Mike. And you? How was the chemistry test?"

He let out an exaggerated groan. "Man! It was a killer! But thanks for the information about the Tutoring Learning Center. Those folks are super helpful."

"Glad to hear it. How's lacrosse going?"

Focusing on this topic brought genuine excitement to his voice. "We're going to Madison this weekend. They're really good, but if we play well, I think we have a chance."

I decided to suggest the open governor position. "So, Mike, has anyone said anything to you about the government position that has come open?"

He nodded, telling me that his community advisor had encouraged him to apply. I seconded that suggestion, and Mike beamed. I told him I'd put his name on the ballot and wished him luck in the election.

Two weeks later, Mike sat in on his first government meeting. He had won the election and was thrilled about the chance to participate.

The following year, he ran for another position in the organization and was elected recreation representative. Through that role, he got involved with the health promotion and wellness department. He enjoyed it so much that he changed his major to health promotion.

At the end of the school year, we had our hall government closure activity, where we shared what we had learned as a group during the year. Between laughing at stories of how not to start a fire at camp and how misspelling words in publicity signs can be an intentional ploy to get people to pay attention and attend a program, Mike had a turn to speak. He told the group how he had learned that if you're going to plan a softball game, using pizza boxes as the bases wasn't a great idea, especially on a windy day, and how he had learned that I always kept a candy stash in my office. A few of the members laughed, and those who hadn't stopped by as frequently scowled jokingly at their loss. Afterward, I was back in my office, working on end-of-the-year paperwork. I heard something being slid under my door. I looked down to find a small white envelope with my name scrawled on the front. It was a thank-you card. As I read it, I found myself reaching for that same box of Kleenex I had given to students over the year.

Dear Kris,

Although at times I haven't been your most outstanding
resident, I want to thank you for all you've done. Getting caught at the
beginning of my freshman year was probably the best thing that ever
happened to me. Since meeting with you that day, I've changed a lot
and for the better. More often than not, I've found myself attracted to
positive activities more than the negative. I'm not going to say that it's
been easy, but the journey has beenrewarding. Last week I received a
thousand-dollar scholarship for my grades and involvement as well as
the Dean's Award for Outstanding Sophomore in Health Promotion and
Wellness. So I just wanted to let you know how grateful I am for your
steering me in the right direction. And thanks for being the most fun
and approachable Hall Director I've ever known.

Sincerely,
Mike

As I wiped my tears, I thought, "This is really why I do my job."

CANINE INTERVENTION

BY
C. RYAN AKERS

A wise person once told me that things always have a way of working out. This mantra could not be proven more than in the following true story. I was two months from graduating from a reputable student affairs program. The NASPA and ACPA annual conferences were fast approaching. I was a picture of organization as I prepared vigorously for job placement at both conferences. My fellow student affairs graduate students were in awe of my preparation and readiness for job interviews. Actually, they probably believed that I was obsessively over-prepared. I had two file boxes neatly organized with résumés and information about each school and thank-you note stationery. I was determined to be the first member of my cohort to get a job. I interviewed at NASPA for several positions and received positive feedback resulting in two on-campus interviews.

Two weeks later, I was off to ACPA. There I interviewed with a highly regarded institution in the Southeast (referred to as Oakley University). I wanted to stay in the Southeast. It was imperative that I nail this interview. I prepared rigorously. I was confident going into the interview because the hiring authority contacted me prior to the conference to set up the interview. They wanted me first, and that felt good.

A couple of weeks later, I learned that I would be one of six applicants invited to Oakley's campus for an interview. Again, I prepared at a feverish pace. As a way of motivating myself, I arrived two days early and looked around town for a place to live. I was confident, excited about my surroundings, and hopeful that I would get the job at this glorious institution. Bring on the interview!

The interview process was peculiar. Several candidates interviewed on the same day. We followed a rotation schedule and had six different interview sessions, including a presentation. To make things even more interesting, all of the candidates had to eat lunch together (talk about indigestion). At the end of the day, I left thinking I had a great chance at the job. To be safe, over the next couple of weeks, I applied for other jobs and arranged four campus interviews.

Puzzled that, about two weeks prior to graduation, I still had not heard from Oakley University, I e-mailed the hiring authority and nervously awaited the response. Later that day, I received the usual rejection: "We had a large number of applicants, but we have decided to offer the position to another candidate." I must admit, I was crushed. I felt like someone had just kicked me in the stomach. But always displaying resilience, I decided to contact the hiring authority for an explanation so that I could learn from this experience and make improvements for future interviews. The answer I received was that I was a "great candidate," and that I had done nothing wrong in the interview. They basically had to draw straws in order to select. Although disappointed, I could move on. I had other job leads. At the end of the call, I expressed an interest in any future openings at Oakley. Case closed. Or was it?

The next day, I received an overnight FedEx package. My name and address were handwritten on the package, and it was from Oakley University. I expected to open the package and find the official letter of denial. To my surprise, I found a contract offering me the position I so desperately wanted. As I read the terms of the agreement, tears came to my eyes. I read, "Your signature on this contract indicates that you accept the terms of employment." I was asked to sign the contract and FedEx it back, as my start date was a mere three weeks away.

Somewhat confused, but elated, I sat down in my living room to compose myself. My persistence and hard work had paid off, and I had the job at Oakley after all. Was the conversation the previous day just a test to see if I really wanted the position? Was I the second choice when the first choice declined? Either way, I did not care. I had a job...not just a job but the one that I wanted.

I e-mailed the hiring director that I was not sure what happened, but that I was extremely excited and looked forward to starting my new job at Oakley. I said that I would be in the area the next weekend to look for a place to live. I then called my landlord and informed him that I could be out of my apartment within two weeks. I telephoned both of my professors to let them know that I had the job that I wanted. Word spread quickly, and I had several congratulatory e-mails waiting when I got back home. I then called two of the apartment companies near Oakley and set up times to sign a lease. I had covered all of my bases, with the exception of one, which was to decide what to do about the other campus interviews that I had scheduled. Later that day, as the responsible candidate is taught to do, I canceled them so the schools would have time to interview other candidates. Over the weekend, I began the arduous task of packing all of my belongings.

The following Monday afternoon, I received an e-mail from the hiring authority that simply said, "Ryan, there must be some mistake. Please call me as soon as possible so that we can discuss this." I immediately called and was informed that the office had made a mistake. There was another candidate with the same first name in the search process, and when the office staff was told that the school was going to hire Ryan, they thought it was me. Apparently, there was no clarification of which Ryan was being hired. So, they printed out a contract with my name on it and wrote my name and address on the FedEx form. The authority said he was sure that I could understand the miscommunication, and he wished me luck with my job search.

The weeks that followed involved extreme frustration and a growing contempt for our field. With the exception of graduation, there was not much good news. My classmates began to accept positions. I started receiving rejection letters for position after position. I grew extremely angry, and began looking for positions outside of the field.

Over the Fourth of July break, I was so consumed with my job search and so frustrated by it that I decided to spend time alone, away from my family, so that I could reflect on my life and my future. Now, I recognized that not only was I frustrated, I was depressed. Things just weren't working out. I continued to apply for positions. Reality was setting in. I had a master's degree in the field and could not get a job, and the optimal hiring season was ending.

Over the holiday, I watched over my grandparents' house. I was armed with a steady supply of résumé paper, videos, and a negative attitude. For the first time since deciding that a career in college administration was for me, I became disgusted with my choice of professions. I began to think that I wanted nothing to do with this field.

One day, my two dogs started barking. As I searched for the cause, I heard a very loud panting sound. I opened the front door and found a solid white bulldog on the doorstep. The poor thing looked like he was on his last legs. If he could have spoken, he surely would have asked for several rounds of ice water, as it was nearing 100 degrees outside. I gave the dog some water and food. He had no collar and no identification. I called my grandparents to ask them if they had ever seen a white bulldog around the neighborhood, but they had no idea to whom he might belong.

Because of my affinity for man's best friend and the dog's affinity for a seemingly endless supply of cold water and food, the dog and I became friends over the next three days. I explained to him my career dilemmas and expressed my frustrations. He simply sat and listened. He followed me everywhere around the house and took my mind off the horrible job search process. Then my new friend disappeared, never to be seen again. The very night he disappeared, I received a phone call and was offered a job. I immediately said yes, even though I was informed I had a few days to think it over. Curiously, the mascot at this institution was none other than a solid white bulldog.

Whenever I look back over this experience, I remember that things always have a way of working out. I moved to a new city, had a great job, surrounded myself with an incredible set of friends and colleagues, and got accepted into a doctoral program in student affairs administration. I am sure that when I hang that diploma on my next office wall, not far away will be the framed contract sent to me from Oakley. I have used it as a motivational tool, and have shared my example in classes about the craziness of a job search.

I now appreciate the trials I went through with this job search. I am grateful for where I have gone professionally and now have a renewed faith in our field. For that I say thank you, Oakley University.

SMALLER SHOWERS

BY
JIM D. HARDWICK

State University (SU), where I started my career in higher education, had a longer history as an agriculture college than as a state university. As a land-grant institution, SU still had all of its agriculture research barns, test crop fields, and livestock arenas. While the admissions staff reminded prospective students of the academic excellence found in the university's non-agriculture majors like architecture, engineering, pharmacy, computers, and business, the long-standing reputation as an agriculture college tended to overshadow the state university label.

Despite SU's solid academic reputation, the university was often overshadowed by Research University (RU), located up the highway. SU was perceived as the "poorer cousin" of RU. Serious students in the state were frequently encouraged to seek a "better" education at RU, while students interested in agriculture or earning a college degree before returning to their family farms were encouraged to attend SU. The strong academic programs at SU were perceived as lagging behind stronger academic programs at RU. Also, RU did not have the agriculture research barns rumored to give SU a "farm" smell when the wind blew from the wrong direction. When it came time for summer orientation, the decision to have the parents tour campus on the back of flatbed trailers reinforced the agricultural feel.

The staff at SU constantly fielded questions comparing SU with rival RU. The SU staff always felt like it had to defend the quality of the education and student life at the institution.

After one particularly hot day of summer orientation, I was with a small group of parents in the common lounge of one of SU's high-rise residence halls. The mother of a prospective student launched into a long narrative about our rival institution. "My oldest daughter went to the Research University up the highway," she told the other parents. "I think she received a much better education at RU than my youngest daughter is ever going to receive here at SU."

Remembering that I introduced myself as a residence hall director, the mother asked me for my opinion on a problem her oldest daughter had living in a residence hall suite at RU. "Every morning when she got up to get ready for school, she would find her suitemate having sex with a man in their shower stall. How

55

can your staff at SU guarantee that my youngest daughter won't have the same problem in your residence hall suites?"

As the rest of the parents looked expectantly at me for my response, I put on my best orientation smile and responded, "Easy—our shower stalls are smaller." The laughter from the other parents made it the perfect ending to the day.

THE PARACLETE

BY

TIMOTHY D. SHAAL

I write this story during my last semester as a graduate student. Soon I will enter the world of student affairs. While I look forward to having a positive impact on the lives of students, at times self-doubt takes control.

Sometimes this work can be thankless, but then I consider the paraclete. The concept of the paraclete is both spiritual and grueling. On the one hand, in Christianity, the paraclete is known as the Holy Spirit or Comforter. On the other hand, the Greek army used a paraclete as a model for warfare. This was a model where two soldiers paired together to fight the enemy. As they fought, they stood back to back, defending and protecting their peer. In either view, the importance of the second being is vital. In a spiritual sense, a person might look to a higher being for comfort or strength in time of need. In ancient Greek warfare, the soldier looked to his brother in arms for safety and personal protection. He trusted his partner with his life.

Why do I reference the paraclete? What relevance does this have for student affairs? Let me explain. Recently, I attended a two-day retreat at a rural campsite. Our residence life professional staff retreats twice a year, once at the beginning of each new academic semester. We play games, complete work, eat, tell stories, and laugh.

As the retreat began to wind down, I found myself enjoying the company of my peers. I realized that during the hectic semester, I lose contact with my fellow hall directors. Our schedules fill, and we fail to take time for each other. I pondered this and began to realize the many ways my colleagues have become a paraclete for me. Most important, I remembered how they supported me at a time when I lost the strongest, most faithful paraclete in my life.

In April 2004, I received a phone call that drastically changed my life. My father had entered the hospital for surgery. Complications arose. My mother called because the complications were serious. I raced home to see my father, my paraclete. I used to call him once a week to hear his voice and seek his advice. My father was a minister. For me, my father fulfilled both roles of the paraclete. While I was growing up, he cared for me when I wrecked my bike, and he also provided spiritual guidance. He was the epitome of the paraclete, both physical and spiritual.

As I sat with my father, I knew that the situation was grave. Little did I know that this day would be my last with him. After his passing, I was stunned and slowly began the long process of healing. Part of the process came in the form of a big red school van. At his viewing, I walked outside to get some fresh air and clear my head. As I looked down the street, I saw a 14-passenger van approach. I knew this van well, as I had driven it many times. It was owned by our residence life office. Out of this van came several of my colleagues, along with my resident assistant staff. At that moment, I realized that I had many paracletes. These people would be my support and protection during my time of need.

They did more than show their support by attending the viewing. They covered duties, closed my hall, and handled student requests. They even found the time to see that I had a basket full of candy, baked goods, and snacks upon my return to campus.

Ultimately, I share this story so that you understand the true nature of the paraclete. It is not just an idea particular to spirituality or warfare. We should not look only to a religion or a history book to understand this concept. It is caring, sharing, understanding, helping, supporting, listening, guiding, and leading. It is feeling and doing. It is being a part of the whole. It is student development. It is support and challenge. It is, very simply, student affairs. As the name of our profession implies, we must be about the affairs of our students. Ultimately, being a paraclete is about empowering students to find their way when they do not know which way to go and being there for them, and for each other, when we need each other the most.

HAVING TROUBLE SLEEPING

BY

JIM D. HARDWICK

When I was a residence hall director in graduate school, I was frequently up late at night and would wander across the lobby from my apartment to my hall office. During one of these late-night trips, I noticed a resident, Mary, who, for the past several nights, had been in the main lobby past midnight. Not letting an opportunity go by to strike up a conversation with a resident, I asked Mary why she was up so late.

She replied that she was having trouble sleeping. She was coming down to the lobby late at night so she could go outside the residence hall to smoke. Sensing that the conversation should not end there, I realized I could ask Mary about her smoking or why she wasn't sleeping. I chose to ask her why she was having trouble sleeping.

She told me that she was having nightmares. She said that the nightmares were the same each night. The nightmares repeated something bad that had happened to her before she came to college.

As a student affairs educator, you come to know when you are on the edge of a conversation where the student disclosure will require a meaningful and thoughtful response. I can remember looking at Mary, thinking how exhausted she looked. The burden of the nightmares was clearly taking a toll. I knew the answer to my next question was part of a conversation that needed to happen. I asked her what had happened before she came to college.

In a quiet voice, Mary told me that she had been raped. Stunned, I asked her if she knew who had raped her. In an even quieter voice, she told me that it was her father. The tears started to flow down her face as she replayed the incident. She told me that her father had wanted to have sex with her before she went to college. She said her father told her that he wanted to have sex with her before any boy at college could.

The tears soon turned to quiet sobs. In gasps of air between the sobs, she told me about the start of her nightmares. The nightmares began when she learned that her father was coming to visit her at college in two weeks. As a punctuation mark, she blurted out, "I don't want to have sex with him again."

All of the training I had as a residence hall director came back to me. I asked her if she would like to talk to a counselor about her nightmares, the rape, or her father. She said that she would like to talk to a counselor about the rape. I asked her about her class schedule and found a block of time when she would be available to meet with a counselor. I offered to schedule the appointment for her when the counseling center opened and to call her room with the appointment time. She accepted the offer. I asked her if she would like me or another staff member to walk with her to the counseling center, but she said that she would be able to go by herself. I asked her if there was anything else I could do for her that night. She thanked me and told me that she was OK. She thought that after our conversation she would try to go back to sleep. She thanked me for taking the time to ask her why she was having trouble sleeping.

I walked back to the hall director apartment and replayed the conversation with Mary several times in my mind. What if I had stopped asking questions when she told me that she was chain smoking? What if I dismissed her statement that she was having trouble sleeping as typical behavior of a college student? What if I didn't continue with the questions until she had disclosed the rape? What if I had not walked from my hall apartment to the hall office?

At the time, it was an uneasy feeling to know that as a residence hall director I would not be there each time a resident needed help. I had to reassure myself that I had a trained student staff that would provide a safety net to help the residents in our building. I also faced the reality that our residents would find support from other campus resources or other support networks outside of the campus.

One week later, I sat again with Mary in the lobby of our residence hall. This time, it was midday rather than the middle of the night. She had her suitcase packed, and I was sitting with her until her ride came. In the week between our visits, Mary had several appointments at the counseling center. Her mental health deteriorated as her father's visit to campus approached. Given the fragility of her mental state, her counselor recommended a residential facility for her to receive the treatment she needed. Her ride would transport her to a mental-health-care facility. As we waited, she told me that she had not had any trouble sleeping since we had our conversation.

Twenty years later, I can still remember the numbness I felt as a new hall director dealing with incest for the first time. Looking back, I think about how different the conversation would be now. I would want to know if the resident was at risk for taking her own life. I would ask if she was on any medications. I would ask if she had talked to anyone about the incident since it happened. I would be concerned about any evidence that was preserved from the incident. I would ask about her contact with her father since the incident. I would explain to her how to obtain a restraining order from the court. I would talk to her about reporting the incident to law enforcement. I would offer to contact the on-call counselor. I would not want to let her walk off alone. I would talk to her about calling a friend who would meet us in the lobby and offer her a place to stay until her appointment at the counseling center.

In this profession, we need to take the time for students. We need to stop, listen, and care. As student affairs professionals, we need to be present for them and listen to their stories. We may not have all the right answers or do all the right things, but listening is a place to begin. Not every story has a problem we can fix. When a story does include a problem, we need to remind ourselves that there are resources beyond ourselves to help fix it.

ACADEMIC URBAN LEGENDS

BY

SARAH M. MARSHALL

I first heard these stories when I was a student affairs practitioner. I don't know if they are true or who invented them. I'm sure that if they were once based in fact, over the years the stories evolved to include probable embellishments. These are fun, retold stories I have used over the years to articulate a particular point, send a message, or simply lighten the mood at a dinner table.

ONE-QUESTION EXAM

The night before their biology exam, a group of four students sat studying. After what they deemed an appropriate amount of time, one student suggested that they call it a night and attend a friend's party at the neighboring college. In unanimous agreement, the students decided they had studied enough and indeed should reward themselves by attending the party.

The four climbed into a car and drove the 20 minutes to the party. Once there, they overindulged in alcohol and merriment and passed out on the friend's bed. The next morning they overslept, missing the biology exam. Frantic, the students concocted a story to tell their professor. Their version went something like this:

> We needed some more resources to study for our exam, so we decided to study at the other university's library. We were up pretty late studying, and when we went to our car to drive home, we had a flat tire. Because of the late hour, we couldn't get someone to fix it until this morning. We tried to get someone as soon as we could, but we obviously didn't get back to campus in time for the exam. We are ready. We studied all night. Please let us take the exam.

The professor nodded and smiled, giving the students every assurance that indeed he understood. He suggested that the students come back later that afternoon to take the exam. Relieved that their lie worked, the students returned later for the exam. The professor put each student in a separate room and handed out the one-question exam: "Which tire was flat?"

DR. JONES

During finals week at a large university, a frantic student barged into the sociology office, interrupting the department chair's conversation with a faculty member. Addressing both individuals, the student began: Excuse me, has either of you seen Dr. Jones? He teaches my Sociology 101 class, and it is very important that I speak with him. I simply cannot take the final exam today. I have an emergency, uh...yeah, an emergency, and I cannot take the exam. He knows me very well. After all, I am one of his top students. I attend every class and participate despite the large class size. I'd never make up an excuse not to take the exam. It's just that something unavoidable has come up. I'm sure he'll understand. Can one of you tell him?

The department chair took down the student's name and promised to give it to Dr. Jones. After the student left the office, the department chair slid the paper across his desk to the female faculty member. Smiling, he commented, "Dr. Jones, it seems that despite a semester of 'regular class attendance' and 'active participation,' your 'top' student fails to recognize you."

LEAVING YOUR PLATFORM: GROUNDING LESSONS ON A MOVING TRAIN

BY

SCOTT C. BROWN

Nine years ago, I took a train. Nine years ago, my wife and I were expecting our first daughter. Nine years ago, I met a girl named Maggy.

Although I am extroverted by any measure (some would argue pathologically), when I travel, I talk to nobody. It seems with everything going faster, faster, faster, the downbeats and respites that were built into our lives have been virtually erased. This is the one place where the relentless pace of our student affairs work relents. Protected in the shroud of travel, I still can find asylum, refuge, and sanctuary to read without feeling I should be doing something else. I also have the time to reflect in my journal.

On the train, I sat next to a grandmother and her granddaughter. They had been traveling far. The granddaughter was growing restless, having long exhausted the amusements she had brought and the conversation her traveling partner offered her. I could tell that she was ready to do something else. Despite my earnest attempts to remain in my own world, the girl got me to talk. I put down my book, knowing the story that was about to be told had to be more interesting than the story I was reading. Her name was Maggy. We talked about her trip. We talked about her school. She offered me some of her ham sandwich. Being a graduate student at the time, I took it.

Because I was anxious about becoming a parent, I asked if she had any particular advice about raising girls. Maggy quickly and succinctly reeled off her suggestions. I knew that what I heard was something I probably didn't want to forget, so I asked her if she would write down her advice in my journal. In her uneven, 10-year-old's handwriting, she wrote: "Maggy's Advice for Scott and Anne-Marie for their new daughter:

> 1. Spend time with her (if you have to go away, call every day and write).

> 2. If you have to go away for a long time (two weeks or more), when you get home, take her out (to a game, shopping, movie theater, amusement park, swimming) for a day— just you and her.

3. Pictures. If she creates anything, take a picture. Put pictures and papers together to create a book you can show her and your grandchildren.

4. If she gets a bad grade, lightly push her to do better. Any other questions, write to Maggy at…"

Maggy and her grandmother got off at a stop shortly thereafter. They turned and waved, and the train moved on. Quickly and quietly they came into my life, quickly and quietly they left.

To be honest, I probably wouldn't recognize Maggy if I passed her on the street today, but I recognize her in my life. Since then, we have had two daughters and a son. As they get older, I find myself going back to the simple and clear directives in her remarks: Maintain a presence even in your absence, and don't let perceived limitations of time and space excuse you from this; what kids produce is valuable and memorable; believe that their best is good enough and never stop helping them find that for themselves; and it's not just what you do but why you do it.

But my interactions with Maggy were meaningful not only as a parent but as an educator as well. Some things that become meaningful inspire nations and roil the souls of a people; their power amplifies with scrutiny. But there are also more subtle moments of meaning, moments that are small, delicate pictures not meant to carry the weight of a heavy and ornate frame, moments that decay if you try to study them too closely or too often. But by completely leaving my own world, even with a child, I have returned to view it in a different light.

Indirectly, Maggy helped me formulate an answer to the question, "Why do you work with students?" She provided me with something that enlarges and deepens when I come back to visit it. It's the type of lesson that provides a small, consistent source of light to illuminate those parts of our lives we may have never seen or have simply walked over. Our work is a glorious landscape dotted with such meaningful moments. The true paychecks of our profession are the awkward thanks of a grateful student or an unsolicited voicemail bursting with the grand news of a breakthrough.

Why did Maggy make me think of our student affairs work? Being an educator, I realize that it is not coincidental that two words that shape our work can trace their etymological lineage to helping children: "educator" and "pedagogy." "Educate" comes from the Latin *educare*, which means "to rear" and "to lead out." "Pedagogy" comes from the Greek *pais* "child" and *agagos* "leader." The core words for our work have their roots in a relationship that is almost parent-like to students. But sometimes it is the other way around. Sometimes it is losing sight of our small role in a grander story. It's trite but true; sometimes it is not what we teach children, but what they teach us. The educator "gets educated." I now know that if I remember to attend to the small things, as time marches on, maybe it won't march right over me. I think I have more questions.

My train ride left me with a very strong impression. Sometimes life's lessons come from a class. Sometimes they come from a book. Sometimes they come from adversity. And sometimes they come from a 10 year old with a ham sandwich.

LOAFING AROUND

BY
CLIFFORD E. DENAY JR.

Depression is rampant in the winter months north of the 45th parallel. Snow and sadness surround me. As a licensed professional counselor at North Central Michigan College in Petoskey, Mich., I am often called upon to help students struggling with the midwinter blues. It's "cabin fever" time. I'm never bored. The lineup is constant and consistent.

So the call wasn't a surprise at all. "Cliff, I'm worried about Jane. She's our new work-study student. She looks awful. I'm no expert, but I think she's really depressed. I can't get her to smile. She isn't doing her work. She's just loafing around. You know, this won't work at all. We have things to do here. And whenever I try to talk to her, she ends up crying. I'm at my wits' end. I can't help her. I asked her if she'd be willing to talk to you. I was amazed when she said yes. What do you think?"

"Will she come now?" I asked.

Silence. Then, "She said she could come right now if you're available."

"Please send her over," I softly replied. "We'll talk."

Jane came in with a tear-streaked face. "Hey," I said. "What's happening? You look like you've had a hard day and it's not even lunchtime." I usually use humor as an assessment tool. If I can get a client to smile or laugh in the first few moments of our meeting, I know the situation isn't entirely hopeless.

"I don't want to be here," Jane replied.

"Here?" I asked. "As in my office?"

"No," she said. "Here, as in at this college. This is the wrong school for me. I keep telling my parents, but they won't believe me. I have no interest in any of my classes. I'm doing horribly, and I feel awful because I'm usually a good student. Have you looked at my high school grades? I kicked butt there. Here, I skip class a lot. That's why I'm flunking. I just don't want to be here. I'm wasting my parents' money."

"Do your parents know how you feel? Are they willing to consider a different school?"

"They say I have to 'prove' myself here first. When I get the grades, they'll let me go where I really want to go. I'm stuck here." Jane talked a long time. She thanked me for listening to her, something no one else seemed willing to do.

Eventually, I sensed an opening. "Jane," I said, "I believe all of us have a 'mental picture album' tucked away in our brains. Our albums have 'pictures' of every life experience. Will you look, right now, in your picture album and find the photograph of you doing something you absolutely love to do? I'm not sure what it is, but you'll recognize it immediately."

"I found it," she said, "The picture I mean. Baking bread. I love baking bread and making desserts, scones, pies, cookies, you know, all kinds of baked goods. I just love it! The only class I like this semester is my baking class."

"Do your parents know?" I asked again.

"Yes, but they don't think I can make a living baking bread. They say I need to find a real job."

I love to bake, too. I told Jane about the kinds of breads and sweets my hands have created through the years. I told her stories about my mother's skills in the bread pan and how, in her later years when she got too sick to bake, she taught my father how to knead the dough. Mom taught Dad to be patient while the yeast worked. I didn't know it at the time, but they both taught me the importance of using my hands when my heart and soul faltered, when the dark days of depression tried to settle in. To this day, I knead homemade dough and shape beautiful free-form loaves whenever I feel depression tugging on my sleeve.

I told Jane she could make a lot of money as a professional baker. She listened with anticipation. I could see hope in her eyes. "Jane," I said, "I have a favor to ask of you."

"Does it have anything to do with baking?" she replied. A smile danced in her eyes.

"How did you know?" I laughed back. "You told me you were baking scones in your next class, right?"

"Yes!" she answered, beaming. "Orange-lemon with a crunchy crust. You'd love them!"

"Actually, I haven't met a scone I didn't love. Would you be willing to drop one off for me after class, you know, as a favor for a starving counselor?" Now, we were both laughing out loud. It felt good.

"I haven't laughed in a long time," Jane said. "I'm glad I came over. And, yes, I'll bring you a fresh scone on Monday."

"There's one more thing I'd like to ask you to do. Would you be willing to do one more favor, this time for your mom and dad?"

"You want me to bake enough scones for them, too, don't you?"

"You're reading my mind," I replied. "Now you're the counselor." We laughed again.

"Yes," I said. "I want you to show them how important baking is to you and how good you are at it already. Will you do that for me, for them?"

"Yes, I absolutely will. Thanks for the idea."

The still-warm scone melted in my mouth that Monday afternoon. And, two weeks later at our next appointment, Jane brought in fresh "country white" bread, just out of the oven. To complete the unexpected treat, she presented butter, peanut butter, and jam, just in case I wanted to make a full-blown sandwich. We talked about the culinary arts schools that she had thoroughly researched. She told me of her plans to visit one of them over spring break. "It'll cost a lot more than North Central," she said.

"You're worth it," I replied. "Right?"

"You bet I am!" she said.

I saw no further signs of depression in Jane. Her campus supervisor reported a "complete change in her attitude." She told me she'd be transferring in the fall. I guess my hands-on approach worked.

Getting students back into familiar and active routines can be the first step in helping them climb out of a depressive mood. In this case, the only additional sessions Jane "kneaded" were in her baking class.

LOOKING OUT TO GET YOU OR LOOKING OUT FOR YOU?

BY

WILLIAM E. O'DELL

As a hall director overseeing a building of more than 300 first-year residents, it sometimes feels like I'm more of a disciplinarian than an educator. Some students I see casually in the dining commons, relaxing in the lounges, or attending programs. Others I see repeatedly sitting across from my desk for various reasons: noise violations, roommate problems, sports in the hall, and alcohol violations. Did I mention I see these few repeatedly? As much as I try to instill the significance of living in a community, respecting others and themselves, and taking responsibility for their actions, it just doesn't seem to sink in. This often leaves me wondering if I am actually helping these students.

One semester, a repeat offender, Kevin, was making frequent trips to my office, and I was making just as many up to his room. Kevin seemed to get caught for violating just about every policy or community standard. To name a few, he was loud at 4 a.m. He initiated naked shower fights that ended up with towel-snapping races down the hallway. He smoked where he shouldn't. He came in intoxicated and belligerent. Underage, he had beer in his room and had many noise violations.

One day, Kevin sat in my office and we talked about his most recent policy violation. He told me that he wanted to go home and not return. I assumed his decision had something to do with the amount of time that he was spending in my office. Upon further questioning, he told me his parents were divorcing. He didn't feel like he was really fitting in at school and had fallen behind in his classes. Recognizing that I could help, I responded, "You know, leaving school doesn't solve your problems. There are other ways and resources to help you." Together we worked out a plan to see a counselor to talk about his parents and made phone calls to his professors to set up individual appointments to discuss his classes. I encouraged him to get involved in a few student organizations.

The next day, Kevin's father called me. Kevin had called home to tell them about our conversation. His father was very pleased to know that his son was going to stay in school at least through the end of the semester. He told me that he and his wife supported any further conversations I wanted to have with his son. What a nice surprise to receive a positive parent phone call!

I met with Kevin again to ask how the meetings had gone with his professors. He let me know that things really weren't as bad as they seemed, and that he was thinking about classes for next semester. I leaned over and told Kevin how proud I was that he was making those steps on his own. I went on to say that even though most students in trouble think that my staff and I are out to get them, in reality, helping students is our main goal. I don't know if I told him this to convince myself or him. Kevin smiled, held out his hand as he got up to go, and said, "I never thought about it as if you guys were out to get me. I've always thought that each time I sit in your office, you always seem more like you are looking out for me." I smiled and thought, "I am, Kevin. That's exactly what I am doing." I shook his hand and said, "Thank you!"

THE PROMISE OF SERVANT LEADERSHIP

BY

ANN MARIE MALLOY

I had my daily lesson in servant leadership this afternoon. As usual, it came from my students, who are my most important teachers. This lesson started at the pizza party for faculty sponsors and student leaders of our campus student organizations. The Muslim students, who are fasting for Ramadan, brought beautiful figs, bread, and honey for all of the others at the luncheon even though they themselves were not eating. Through their generosity, I was reminded of the important qualities of restraint and sacrifice.

After the luncheon, the president of the Students for Christ group went up to two of our Muslim students and offered to help them and their newly formed association in any way he could. Thus, I witnessed another characteristic of true servant leadership, tolerance. The Muslim students who founded the Muslim Student Association (MSA) in our college this year have done so in a national environment that has been extremely distrustful of them. Yet when they chose their faculty sponsors for the MSA, the first person they asked was Jewish and the second was me, an Irish Catholic. Likewise, when our student activities office and humanities faculty cosponsored a lecture series called "A Season of Non-Violence," featuring Arun Gandhi as the keynote speaker, the Muslim students from Pakistan were most anxious to meet him despite the conflicts between the Muslims and Hindus in India and Pakistan.

In his 1970 essay, "The Servant As Leader," which was reprinted in *The Power of Servant Leadership*, Robert Greenleaf wrote that the best test of servant leadership is "do those served grow as persons; do they, while being served, become healthier, wiser, freer, more autonomous, more likely themselves to become servants?" This quotation reminds me of all of the lessons I have learned from my students during the last 18 years as a faculty member in the arts and humanities at our large Midwestern community college. For instance, last semester a young student shared the excitement and wonder in his discovery of Sophocles' play *Antigone*. He described it as a cautionary tale warning of the pitfalls of arrogance and hubris. His insight and enthusiasm reminded me to be humble in the presence of complex human relationships.

A young honors student described her college experiences with global humanities as helping her understand "how connected the world is, how we all have helped each other, how we all should help each other." Her words celebrate the important quality of community building through servant leadership and showed her understanding of how the world has been constructed through complicated cross-cultural negotiations over long periods. One of our young soldiers who was attempting to take an online art appreciation class from a tent in Kuwait experienced these cultural complications firsthand when his studies were interrupted by repeated information and energy blackouts during the war. Sometimes the students exemplify true heroism as they face difficult and overwhelming challenges in their personal lives. I learn so many important lessons from these amazing people. In one case, I learned the power of love as I witnessed a lovely young mother complete the semester with a B even though her 3-year-old daughter had been diagnosed with leukemia. Indeed, from all of the students who succeed in their college studies despite poverty, disabilities, addictions, or heavy work responsibilities, I have learned the importance of courage and perseverance.

Awareness, listening, healing, gratitude, compassion, stewardship, persuasion, empathy, and commitment to a mission greater than ourselves are other qualities Greenleaf describes as essential to servant leadership. The students help me remember these every day. However, the most important lesson of all comes from the family and friends of my student Leanna, who was murdered several years ago. This lesson also resonates in the life of my former student, Justin, who died last year at the age of 26 from an epileptic seizure, as well as in the painful struggle of Diana, who recently died of Crohn's disease at the age of 24. From them I have learned that hope is stronger than history.

David Smith says, "To be a teacher...requires that I face my Teacher, which is the world as it comes to me in all of its variegation, complexity and simplicity. When I do this, I face myself, and see myself reflected in the faces of my brothers and sisters everywhere" (p. 24). The students are "The Teacher" that I face every day. They are the education that I profess to serve.

References

Smith, D. G. (1999). *Pedagon*. New York: Peter Lang Publishing.

Spears, L. (1998). *The Power of Servant Leadership*. San Francisco: Berrett-Koehler Publishers.

EMOCEAN

BY

BECCA MINTON

While I worked to obtain my degree in student affairs administration, I served as a graduate assistant in the Office of Gender Issues Education Services. Our office counseled students who are lesbian, gay, bisexual, transgender, and/or questioning their sexual identity and survivors of sexual assault. Most of my responsibilities involved conducting proactive educational programs. While I enjoyed the programming aspect of my position, meeting with students was when I felt the most fulfilled.

Many times, the students I met with were in some kind of crisis. They were dealing with complex issues, such as coming to terms with their sexuality or beginning to accept that they had been sexually violated. The appointments with students were never happy or lighthearted. However, I was always incredibly grateful to be a part of their lives, even for a short time.

One winter break, while on the Outer Banks of North Carolina, I took the opportunity to reflect on the students I had met that semester. Though none of them had ever met one another and each came to me with very different issues, I realized that there was a significant commonality in all of them: their immense courage. As I watched the waves of the ocean come in that day, I realized there might be a way I could articulate their amazing courage.

I barely feel as though words can come close to expressing my appreciation to those students. They inspired me, and for this, I can only say how incredibly fortunate and honored I feel to have been a part of their support network.

The following poem is for them—for their brave voices to be heard and known.

EMOCEAN

Clumsy silence befalls the room where two people sit,
Its too-big feet awkwardly shuffling about,

While somewhere, miles away, the bud of a wave
Is fighting to form itself amidst the chaos of the bumbling whitecaps that
surround it.

Back inside the room, both people are extraordinarily aware
Of the phenomenon that has brought them together for this time.

One of them has a gashing wound that she does not have the strength to hide anymore
She has come for help.

Her body sits, folded into itself,
Fighting to stay small, stay hidden.

Outside, the baby wave grows up a little while it flails helplessly about
Being pummeled by the shoulders of bigger waters.

The room is throbbing with silence
Although no words are being spoken,
Both people are sharing in a certain and significant communion.

But her mouth stays locked shut, while Trepidation minds the key.
She is brutally aware that once the words she has inside are uttered aloud
Trepidation will swallow the key into his dark belly of Truth,
Where it will be permanently irretrievable.

The wretched words of truth will infuse life into Trepidation's children: Shame
and Anguish.

Eyes meet again and stay joined for a time.
"See?" one set tells the others,
"You're not as isolated as the cold shelter of your mind would have
you believe."

Outside, the lonely wave toddles its way through icy waters
Mindful of glaciers pushing it away
Building in strength as it perseveres.

Inside, the words have finally jimmied the lock of her mouth open.
At first, her voice is soft, as if the words themselves are in disbelief that they have escaped
The warm jail that failed to suffocate and terminate their existence

Gradually, her voice gathers power with certainty
Soon, the words begin to eagerly spike through the air.

Outside, the wave is beginning to smile with excitement
It can tell the journey is almost complete because it feels the prickly seagull feet on its back.
Its crest forms from adrenaline, and it becomes huge

For a time, the room is electric with emotion
As the words continue to dart out of her mouth and zigzag anxiously about.

Finally, she stops to breathe.

Indeed, Shame and Anguish are more palpable now,
But something else, previously invisible, is slowly taking shape:

The unmistakable sweetness of Relief.

And as it takes shape, it floods her eyes
And spills into the room in courageous torrents

Outside the window, the wave's form overlaps like a graceful gymnast
And it gallantly and boldly crashes to the shore.

WHEN STUDENTS DIE

BY
PEGGY C. HOLZWEISS

Even though I was a member of the Texas A&M University bonfire advisory committee in 1999, I found out like everyone else—on the local news at 7 a.m. Five hours earlier, a 55-foot-tall bonfire had collapsed, taking numerous students with it. By the time I saw the live television report, several students were confirmed dead and many more were believed to be trapped under the heavy stack of logs.

The reality of what had happened did not penetrate my state of shock until I saw the immense pile of collapsed, twisted lumber. Students had been building the stack through the night for the traditional bonfire. They worked on all five levels of the wedding cake-shaped structure, some as high as 50 feet off the ground sitting in swings, wiring logs together to help make the stack taller and wider. With only a few seconds warning, the stack spiraled south and came crashing down. Students on the north side of the stack were thrown off, while the students on the south side were trapped underneath the full weight of the logs.

No one knew exactly who was trapped. Student groups had signed up to work on the stack that evening, most of them from residence halls. Individual students representing the groups showed up to work the shifts, but no one kept a thorough list of names. By the time I arrived at the site, teams of staff and students were already going through each of the residence halls, trying to account for every resident. Names of those who could not be found were added to a list of the missing.

As I took in the devastating scene, I saw groups of students wordlessly removing heavy logs from the pile. One by one, they walked the logs more than 100 yards in order to clear the area for emergency crews and rescue equipment. This went on for hours. When one group tired, another one immediately took its place. The football team canceled its practice session for the biggest game of the year to help haul logs.

Thousands of other students gathered outside of the taped-off perimeter to offer assistance, grieve, and pray. The perimeter fence became a living memorial as flowers, poems, T-shirts, pictures, and personal notes were left to express the sorrow everyone felt. Staff and student leaders organized a formal vigil in the

77

campus arena for later that evening. The purpose of the vigil was to help the community deal with the tragic event.

Logs were still being removed and bodies were still being found when the vigil began that evening. Buses arrived at the stack site to escort the bonfire student leadership and staff members to the arena. As our group entered the arena, which was filled to capacity, all eyes turned to the young people who served as the bonfire leadership. They were still wearing their hard hats and were covered in the dirt and grime that came with moving logs all day. Not one word was spoken as the group made its way to the floor of the arena. The university president and the student body president delivered moving speeches conveying their feelings of loss and consoling the thousands of people who had shown up to pay their respects.

After the speeches, the stage party began to file off the platform. Under normal circumstances, this would signal to the crowd that it was time to leave. However, on this evening, the crowd did not move or speak. Everyone remained in their seats, not wanting to leave. Then, in one corner of the arena, a small group could be heard singing *Amazing Grace*. The entire arena joined in within seconds. When the song ended, the crowd filed out of the arena without a sound. Our group again boarded the buses, and we returned to the site. The recovery process took 24 hours from the time the stack fell to removal of the last body. In all, 12 students died and 27 were injured.

My only previous experience with death had been the loss of my grandparents. Young people aren't supposed to die! I had entered student affairs so I could work in an energetic learning environment and help students become well-rounded, successful adults. After the bonfire accident, I questioned why I chose the profession. Nothing prepared me for the challenge of providing comfort and guidance to students while trying to come to terms with my own experience of losing young people who were supposed to be doing something fun. The aftermath of the accident drained me emotionally, and for months I felt the need to change careers.

Six years later, I still work at the same institution and I am still in student affairs. I rediscovered my passion for helping young people develop and learn. I wish I could explain what made me stay in the field, but I still do not really know. It is probably the passage of time combined with the small successes I had with students along the way. I still find it hard to relive the memories and images of the accident, and I doubt I will ever feel strong enough emotionally to visit the site or the memorial that honors those we lost.

I am grateful that I was part of this painful experience. Because of the bonfire accident, I had the opportunity to observe the strength of parents. The way they dealt with their personal losses was truly a model of faith and inspiration. I also had the opportunity to witness a large community rally together when it really counted. Differences we were quick to point out just days before the accident faded away with our shared sorrow. Through the tragic deaths of students, I learned something that I could never pick up from a book or class—how to deal with my own feelings of grief and to cherish those I love.

FINDING MEANING BEHIND MY DESK

BY

JENNIFER FONSECA

My office is cozy and decorated to suit my personality. On the wall is a large, gold-framed corkboard covered in organza blue fabric that is smothered with pictures of family and friends. My fish tank is home to Gordo and Methuselah, the last two of the original 10 fish. A burgundy-fringed lamp sits atop a pedestal coffee table (perfect for coffee chats). The small Oriental rug rests under two institutional, yet well-upholstered, chairs. There is an assortment of other homey items, commonly referred to as knickknacks. Even the mouse pad is a miniature version of a Persian rug. It is in this office with a large window overlooking the campus chapel that I do my job. Or is it really where I come to fulfill my calling?

There are many days when I enter my office, pull out my blue high-back executive chair, and go through the 98 e-mails that daily come to my account. In the midst of e-mails, there is the looming task list of 15 items waiting to be crossed off. My desk becomes cluttered with legal pads of notes (and doodles), budget proposals, assessment tools, and a thousand ideas for the programs I want to implement when I get the chance.

Not too long ago, there was a day like this, when I came to work only to be bombarded by the day's demands and supervisory issues. I was exhausted. It was the 15th week of the semester, and I was tired from teaching four sections of our freshman seminar, training three new employees, and putting out a variety of fires. This was the day Katie walked into my office. It was already 5:30 p.m. I was trying to wrap up my day. It was a rare day that I didn't get to hear the 6 o'clock bell chimes as I continued through the myriad of tasks. Katie indicated she just had an "academic question." I did some triage: "Is this something that will take 30 seconds or 10 minutes to answer?" I am not sure why I asked that question. Students think any question they have requires only a brief answer.

I felt too busy to answer her question. I wanted to leave before the bells chimed 6. I was tired. I, I, I. It was all about me, and shouldn't it have been? After all, I worked a 10-hour day; I punched the clock and needed a personal life. It was then that I noticed the puffy, watery eyes. It was then I saw the quick quiver of the lip and frazzled face of an 18-year-old woman whose world looked like it was going to fall apart. I stopped my multitasking, looked straight into Katie's eyes, and asked, "Are you OK? What's wrong?" She began to bravely explain how her younger sister had called to tell her that her parents were divorcing. It was the week before finals, and Katie's world was falling apart around her.

I asked her to sit down and tell me the story. "No, I'm sorry. I know you need to get home. I'm keeping you late," she said. I knew this was a moment that would pass if I did not take time for her. Forget the e-mails, budget proposals, and other paper trails on my desk. The 6 o'clock bell chimes rang as we talked about how she was handling the news and about resources to support her during this time. The Kleenex box felt the tug of Katie's tears. I felt the tug on my heart. Minutes and hugs later, we walked out of the office together. As tired as I was, these are the significant moments. What at first felt like an interruption to my very important work was an opportunity to serve and minister to the heart of a hurting student.

Every day, I walk into my nicely decorated office and find the same pile of papers and problems. I often get discouraged by the lack of progress and the apparently insurmountable obstacles to achieving my goals, and yet every morning I come. I am reminded of a book I once read which described a desk similar to mine, with papers and administrative tasks randomly scattered about. The difference between that desk and mine was the perspective the owner had on the scattering of items: The desk was not just an ordinary oak rectangle with drawers—it was a communion table. That desk was a place where amidst the piles and papers, one would serve others. Each e-mail, assessment grid, project timeline, or change of major form was an opportunity to serve another. The administrative tasks directly affect people, the people I long to serve and develop.

Katie will not be returning next semester; however, I hope the impact of our conversation and the caring heart of an administrative staff member will help give her strength to face the challenges at home. There are other Katies who will never come to my office to share their stories, but each student is touched by the things that arrive on my desk also seeking attention. I choose daily how to perceive the administrative work that greets me. And, when the next opportunity to advise and counsel a student intersects with his or her need for help, I will be grateful to stay late to hear the bells chime.

A STORY OF FOUR IN THE FACE OF ADVERSITY

BY

DIANE WARYOLD, ELIZABETH BALDIZAN, FELICE DUBLON, AND LINDA TIMM

A sense of purpose is a concept that many professionals in student affairs seldom take the time to explore. It is not uncommon for professionals to report that they fell into this line of work when confronted with tough, fundamental questions such as, "Why did you become a dean of students (or a vice president for student affairs, a judicial affairs administrator, a director of housing, and so on)?" And, more important, why does your work matter?

This is a story of four women's journey and how they were brought together through their interest in college student behavior. It is a story of profound sadness and loss and the adversity they faced that solidified their friendship. It is a tale of a trusted sisterhood and an example of the joy and delight that come with discovering the importance of the connections made through our careers and the true purpose of our work. It is the answer to the million-dollar question, "Why does our work matter?"

When ruminating over why four individuals with varied interests and unique personalities would choose a career in student affairs, these four women see several common themes. First, all four were mentored by someone who made a difference in their lives and planted the seed that propelled them into student affairs. Second, all four enjoyed experiences in student leadership and involvement in some aspect of student life during their undergraduate years. Third, they recognized the need to work with people, instead of material objects, and valued family, friends, and interpersonal relationships. Fourth, all four women share a love for students, are intrigued by their wonderfully rich minds, and possess the desire to unearth their passions.

Their paths were strikingly similar but, without divine intervention, close to never intersecting. Diane "Daisy" Waryold and Felice Dublon graduated from the same doctoral program and were mentored by Dr. Melvene Hardee at Florida State University but never overlapped years. Linda Timm and Felice Dublon attended the same high school in suburban Chicago and raised families in the Midwest but do not remember if they ever met then. Elizabeth Baldizan and Felice Dublon were active in NASPA at the same time but never on the same committees. Their lives have been separated by four time zones, and their individuality is custom-made. What these four women did ultimately share was an interest in college student behavior and a need to understand how their roles on campus could influence that behavior.

They met at the Stetson Law in Higher Education Conference more than 20 years ago and eventually played a role in the creation of the Association for Student Judicial Affairs (ASJA). Each served as president of that organization during its formative years. Each year at the ASJA conference, they would run into each other and share stories that only a "besieged clan"—a group that valued each other's campus capers like no other—would appreciate and comprehend. They would sit down with other trusted colleagues and hash out solutions to complex issues, mixing in news about their families and their harried personal and professional lives. The gatherings were brief but essential to sustaining such intense existences where work and a balanced lifestyle were continually works in progress.

Of course, the professional is not easily separated from the personal, and a dean or vice president of student affairs is rarely merely a dean or vice president by day. Although professionals in student affairs constantly struggle to make sense out of the ambiguities that regularly present themselves, there is no ambiguity in understanding what is needed to successfully manage this life. Without family and a trusted sisterhood, none of these four women would have prevailed. In many ways, their friendship is similar to relationships cherished by countless others. They e-mail each other frequently, very often about the nothingness and everythingness of their daily lives, the latest student issue confronting them on campus, or plans for their next visits. When they do see each other, amazingly several times a year, the joy of connecting is palpable. There's a celebration of feasting—imbibing good wine, and eating each other's lovingly prepared concoctions or dining out at the finest restaurants, typically accompanied by nonstop conversation. The four enjoy different permutations of a family and are at peace with each combination.

Suddenly, their friendship was put to the test and their bond was strengthened through a heartbreaking event. Linda's husband, Dale, was diagnosed with a rare form of lung cancer. Dale lost his battle with cancer within months of the diagnosis. Abruptly, ambitions seemed trivial and relationships of the friends indispensable. Daisy knew him best and shepherded the three through each stage of his illness, conveying hope within a context of realism. Linda and her exceptional children, both in their early 20s, allowed access to their grief and the difficult conversations that followed. Linda describes her movement through those early days as "walking in a haze;" yet all agree that her deeply ingrained "deaning" skills kicked into automatic, as she led her colleagues, her family, and her friends through the unfamiliar.

In the year that followed, the four professional acquaintances and now kindred friends saw each other at ASJA, continued a more regular e-mail correspondence, talked by cell phone, and eventually found their way to Linda's home in Indiana for a weekend of stories and remembrances. Like the students that they work with, each changed and has been changed by her experiences. They talked about and cried over Dale's death and recognized that they all owned a part in the continued journey through the grieving process. They acknowledged the growth in their relationship. Had it not been for the initial professional meeting and their shared work in student affairs, they might have missed each other.

In 2004 at the NASPA Annual Conference, on the day that they were slated to leave for home, the four met at a coffee shop in Denver. They spoke about the year, their struggles with change, the intersection of their lives, and the gift that adversity had left them. Linda spoke of the power of divine intervention and the convergence of five lives as a part of a greater plan. The powerfulness of their relationship had crept up behind them, an unplanned influence on professional lives that had been successful precisely because they had each other and had been awakened to the purpose of their journey. In a recent writing, Gary Pavela (LPR, 2005), an admired mentor and valued friend, summed up the importance of teaching students about the value of cultivating friendships and the interconnectedness to others by declaring that "we are what we love." The revered friendship of these four illustrates how true this is.

Although seasoned professionals, these four women continue to seek out the challenges and the educational purpose of their work. They continue to engage countless numbers of students about making good choices and the impact that these choices have on behavior. Student affairs may be something that a young professional falls into without giving it much thought. But as a career, it is ripe with teachable moments about the fragility and value of life. Our professional and personal success is defined by our connectedness to others. No longer a question but rather a declaration, it is crystal clear why this work matters.

References

Pavela, G. (2004). Friendship, fidelity, and academic integrity. *ASJA Law and Policy Report*, Review, No. 154. Retrieved September 30, 2004, from http://asja.tamu.edu

A HEALING JOURNEY

BY

LINDA R. QUALIA

My intention is to write about healing: educators as healers, student development personnel as healers. This concept may offer new perspectives about what we do on a daily basis—how we interact not only with our students but also within ourselves.

In my heart, I am a poet. I enjoy symbols and metaphors. Over the last several years, my path has led me to pay more attention to life and work, to observe my surroundings, and to mindfully listen. I look for meaning in my experience, even in the mysterious, the unexplainable, and the uncontrollable. I address issues of the heart and soul, of connection and intimacy. I often speak in a language of intuition and symbol. Join me for a brief time on this journey into this story, into this sacred space—the heart and soul of our work.

Early in my career as a therapist, as I entered the world of higher education and student development, I experienced a relationship with a student that changed me and my approach to and understanding of my work. The relationship took me into a deep experience of healing. While I was working with this student, she was diagnosed with breast cancer. She invited me to join her on this journey. Initially, she fought hard to beat the disease. At some point, it became clear that she was going to die, and again she allowed me to share her process. I witnessed her open to a new level of healing and acceptance that I find difficult to put into words. She grieved. She rejoiced. She found peace in her connection with her friends. When I received the call that she had died, I wept. She had changed my life by giving me the gift of her vulnerability, letting me into her heart and her soul.

Vulnerability? Vulnerability as a student development professional? As an expert? We want to appear confident and competent, braced against the obstacles and pain of life situations. This is the face we are conditioned to present to the world, and we believe that it is our competence and confidence that make us useful productive, and lovable. Yet I contend that it is the moments of vulnerability that allow others to warm to us and, perhaps more important, allow us to experience compassion for ourselves. When we let down our guard, we show our softness, we express our emotions, our creativity, and what is close to our hearts. This invites people to know us.

When we allow ourselves to connect to others, we, too, must "do our work." We are asked to confront our feelings, beliefs, and values; we must be open to new territory in our personal journeys through life. The conversations we hear may disturb us. They may challenge our internal sense of safety and security. They will, therefore, invite us into an internal conversation—to take our own journey. My discomfort, my concerns for and with students move me deeper into myself and further along my path of growth and psychological and spiritual evolution.

David Whyte (2001), a British poet, speaks eloquently of vulnerability, of risking ourselves, of walking on the "edge" of what is comfortable in our lives, of having a conversation with the unknown; of serving that deeper part of ourselves that longs for expression. I believe it is on this edge that we touch and serve our students.

One student I have been honored to know had been so traumatized in her young life that for many months we sat together in silence before she slowly began to speak the words of her experience. Over time, she began to peel back the layers of her protective emotional and social armor, learning to have compassion for herself rather than to continue abusing herself as others had abused her. At the beginning, her story resided in this silence, and my presence with her in this space proved the conversation necessary to engage her in a deeper level of meaning and of healing. As E. E. Cummings (n.d.) said, "We do not believe in ourselves until someone reveals that deep inside us something is valuable, worth listening to, worthy of our touch, sacred to our touch. Once we believe in ourselves we can risk curiosity, wonder, spontaneous delight or any experience that reveals the human spirit." I challenge us, as educators, to honor ourselves, our students, and our work in this manner.

On the surface, personal counseling may seem different from the work of others in student development. Where we are alike is that we often see students who are in crisis—developmental issues invoke emotionality, volatility, and shame as do the concerns about relationships, depression, anxiety, abuse, and many of the other challenges that lead students to seek counseling. Students often come to us when they are vulnerable, hurting, frightened, and reaching out. Facing us often requires great courage and determination. Yet herein lies the opportunity for touching a person; for healing, because at these moments, we may enter the realm of story. If we are attentive and we listen, we may be privy to a sacred space that touches universal magic and mystery. We have an opportunity to serve.

We all are teachers and healers when we interact with others. What is required of us is to listen; to have an open heart as we listen; to respect the wholeness as well as the vulnerability of ourselves and others; to appreciate, with compassion, the plight of another; to have faith that although we will not always be able to help or fix, we may be serving and honoring a deeper process. It is a simple task, yet profoundly difficult.

We live with the paradox of life: While so much is uncertain, we may also find certainty in the mystery and the awe. I am learning that if I am awake, mindful, and attentive, I will notice the flow and unfailing pattern and endurance of life. I can believe in the resilience of the human spirit.

References

Cummings, E. E. (n.d.). E. E. Cummings quotes from Thinkexist.com. Retrieved January 1, 2005, from http://www.thinkexist.com/English/Author/x/Author_2706_1.htm.

Whyte, D. (2001). *Crossing the unknown sea.* New York: Riverhead Books.

COMMON GROUND

BY

WANDA L.E. VIENTO AND CARRIE E. MEYER

Many students consider their electives "fun" classes. When we enrolled in the special issues class entitled "Lesbian/Gay Issues in Counseling and Development," what we discovered was far from fun. We found a meaningful class, full of self-discovery. The class enrolled student affairs professionals, counseling psychology students, social workers, and a minister. After two classes, we realized how challenging the course would be—in fact, it was close to hell. Each week, emotions were raw for someone in class. Students often cried, some raged, some feared. Little did we know that we would hear about personal experiences in reparative therapy, dating transgender people, anti-gay public speakers, career changes, and our own personal journeys. Our learning went far beyond the classroom. This is our story.

Wanda:
Walking into the classroom, I had no idea how much this course would change my life. It was only the second semester of my doctoral program in student affairs in higher education. After 20 years as a social worker, I needed a change. During my first semester, I took a basic college student development course. As the oldest student in the class, I did not think the traditional models applied to me and often challenged the professor to adapt the models to my life experiences. When he ably did so, I realized that theory was not only useful, it was exciting!

When a graduate assistant position as the coordinator of Lesbian, Bisexual, and Gay (LBG) Student Services opened up unexpectedly in the middle of the semester, that same professor suggested that I apply for the position. I was confused. Why me? I identified as heterosexual. He assured me that my social work background was good preparation. He knew I was in a private practice with LBG-identified partners, had worked with many LBG clients, and had friends who identified as LBG. I applied for the position, interviewed, and accepted the job. I then enrolled in the special issues class to prepare myself further for the job. When the class started, I still questioned whether I was entitled to be there.

Carrie:
I completed my undergraduate studies at a small, private liberal arts college where I joked that I was the only out lesbian on campus. There was not an LBG group on campus, and I did not think that we needed one since I was convinced it would just be me sitting alone in the room, drinking bad punch and eating stale cookies.

When I saw the LBG class in the graduate catalog, I enrolled immediately. At the time, I wanted to be a marriage and family therapist, so the class fit in nicely with my curriculum, but that is not really why it took it. It was simply validating to see a class that dealt with my orientation.

Wanda:
The professor structured the class so that each week two or three people would tell their personal journey stories. I was reluctant to tell my story, feeling that it paled in comparison to some of the heart-wrenching journeys—painful coming-out experiences with family rejections, forced attempts at reparative therapies, years in hiding, and internalized homophobia interfering with self-love. Having heterosexual privileges all my life, I did not feel a right to speak. When I finally did, emotions overwhelmed me as I detailed the homophobic and heterosexist lessons I learned and internalized and the ways that I struggled to deconstruct those earlier teachings in my life.

Although I received positive feedback from most of my classmates, one student continuously challenged me, on personal and professional levels. Carrie was a recent graduate and was working at a blue-collar job. She identified as a lesbian and reinforced many of the typical stereo types—young, tough, masculine, loud. Basically, I saw her as the opposite of me.

Carrie:
I was not excited about the first day of class, but I was happy to be there. The happiness was short-lived, though, when I saw Wanda sitting in the classroom—the straight woman who took "my job." I applied and interviewed for the LBG coordinator graduate assistantship. They hired a straight woman. In my eyes, not only had I lost a fabulous job, but I lost to someone who obviously was not qualified. I had never met her, and I did not like her. She was a straight woman in a job made for a gay person—more specifically, for me.

Wanda:
Three weeks into my new job, I learned that a conservative student group on campus was bringing in an anti-gay speaker. I was unsure about my role and what, if anything, I should do about it. When I went to class that week, I raised the issue. Carrie seemed to challenge me directly. "Well, what are you going to do about it?" she demanded.

Her challenge made me begin to think about what I needed to do. I was not familiar with the campus or the student population yet. With the help of my supervisor, I started to make plans. I reserved a room next to the one planned for the speaker, enlisted LBG-affirmative counselors and ministers from the community to volunteer to be present in that room for students, met with the lesbian, bisexual, gay, and transgender student groups at our university and a neighboring private college, and organized a march to travel through the two campuses. I worked with the local LBG resource center to plan these activities.

The following class, I was proud to report on my progress. To my shock, the very woman who challenged me before now dismissed me. Carrie said, with a laugh, "I don't know why you're doing all this. She has a right to speak, you know." What was going on with her? Why was she treating me this way? She seemed to trigger all of my insecurities about being in this position.

Carrie:
How "out" I was depended on where I was. Although I was out to myself since 17, I had just come out to my family at the age of 23. At work, I drove a forklift, and most of my colleagues were men whose favorite jokes bashed gays. I certainly was not comfortable being out around them. However, since I did not have to hide from my family anymore, when the subject of the anti-gay speaker arose, I ran full-force toward a pride phase. I felt something had to be done. The rejected and bitter side of me thought who better to organize something than the "straight ally" in the LBG office. Besides, it was her job.

To my surprise and dismay, Wanda did it. I had to admit she organized a fantastic event. I had never marched or protested before. This was new to me, and I was scared. I tried to tell myself that I was hiding behind the sign because it blocked both cold and wind, but it was truly because I was scared. I was scared that one of the television cameras would put me on the news, someone at work would see it, and I would have to suffer the consequences. I was scared that one of the onlookers would decide to use a bottle as a weapon. I was scared that some anti-gay type would be at a stop sign as we crossed the street, decide he did not feel like waiting for the "homos" to pass, and I would end up on the underside of a minivan.

I cannot explain why, but I thought I should stick as close to Wanda as possible. Maybe she had done this before and would know what to do if a bottle hit my head. Maybe Wanda's "straightness" would be apparent and therefore all the action would happen toward the back of the line instead of up front with us. Whatever was going through my mind, I stuck to her like glue.

Wanda:
The day of the march arrived and, strangely, Carrie seemed to attach herself to my side. I had arrived at the neighboring campus with candles and signs for the marchers. It was inspiring to see how many people from the community cared. The energy was high, with faculty, staff, and students all in attendance. We left the college under an overcast sky, snaking around snow mounds and slippery sidewalks. A local TV crew was there, interviewing people and filming our progression. With Carrie shadowing me as we walked to our campus, I began to

notice things about her that did not fit with the way I had perceived her earlier. She seemed nervous and would hide her face with her sign every time the cameras were directed toward us. I asked her about that, and she revealed that she was not out at her workplace and feared what would happen to her if she were outed. I asked what made her come to the march then, and she sarcastically blew it off, saying it was for extra credit. In my mind, I thought she was taking a stand for herself and I admired that. I knew she had just come out to her family, and that the class helped prompt her. This glimpse of her vulnerabilities helped me to understand her a little more and forced me to reconsider my initial stereotyped view of her. Beyond that tough exterior, there was a strong, intelligent person frightened by homophobia yet standing up for what she believed in. As an ally, I was trying to do the same thing. I began to think we were not so different after all.

Back in the class, Carrie downplayed the event again. She did not mention her own fears and summed up the event as "a big deal over nothing." For me, the big deal was the speaker's subtle, implicit message that being LBG was not acceptable and that people can and should change their sexual orientation. It was a dangerous platform to be preaching. Still, I learned to see Carrie's sarcasm and tough demeanor as a way of coping. Although somewhat softer now, she continued to be antagonistic toward me—until our final project.

Carrie:
Our final project was to be a visual summary of what we had learned in the class. I brought to class pictures of my straight friends. I passed these pictures around the class and explained that I used to believe all these people were "straight allies." Because they were straight and accepted me as lesbian, I made the assumption that they were allies. I also explained that it was not until I met, chatted with, and learned from Wanda that I realized my friends were not actually straight allies. They were just straight. The class taught me that there is so much more to being an ally than accepting your friend's non-straight orientation. I am not a sentimental person, but I could tell that what I said touched Wanda. She was crying, for Pete's sake! It was my way of apologizing for my behavior and attitude. It was also my way of telling Wanda that I appreciated her.

Wanda:
The final project was an incredible experience to wrap up this class. When Carrie started talking about her friends and then mentioned my name, I braced myself for another challenge. The challenge I encountered was far different from my expectations. I was stunned by what Carrie was saying. Her words overwhelmed me. I could not speak. She asked, almost shyly, if it was OK for her to say those things. I think she left everyone with their mouths hanging open. It was one more way that she made me confront my preconceived ideas about who she was.

Carrie:

All in all, I can chalk it up to immaturity or inexperience, or both, but I did not behave very well towards Wanda. It was obvious that by the end of class I had grown. I am still tough on the outside and nothing will change the way I voice my opinions; however, the class taught me that there are people out there who are willing to work toward a common good for the LBG community. I learned that sometimes these people are heterosexual and these straight allies are valuable to the LBG community. This is the most important thing I gained from this class. Specifically, I learned that Wanda, an older heterosexual, a combination that I thought would be detrimental to the success of the university's LBG resource office, was one of its most valuable assets.

Wanda:

For me, that semester encapsulated how I have come to conceptualize student affairs. My work in the LBG Student Services office was about networking with, advocating for, supporting, and rejoicing in all our students. Both Carrie and I were experiencing our own developmental stages, coming together in the same classroom from varied extremes, yet we both benefited. I had to confront my own stereotypes and preconceptions almost daily, and so did she. From opposite ends of the spectrum, we found common ground, respect, and admiration for each other, which culminated in a treasured friendship. Regardless of our ages or stages, there is a place at the table for all of us, and that is what the student affairs profession symbolizes for me.

An Unexpected Thank You

by

Lori Reesor

One of our campus student organizations created a campus event titled "Faculty and Staff Appreciation Day." As an academic administrator at the University of Missori–Kansas City, I received an invitation. I had the day marked in my calendar but didn't think much about it since I was unfamiliar with the program. A few days before the event, I received another invitation, informing me that I had been nominated by a student. I accepted the invitation, assuming that one of my student leaders was responsible for the nomination.

When I arrived at the program, I was given a folder with information about the event and the letter of nomination. As I pulled the letter out of the folder, I quickly looked at the signature. It wasn't one of my student leaders. I recognized the name, but I could not picture her face. I looked around the room, trying to place her, wondering if she was even there. This is what her letter said:

Dear Sirs:

I am aware that I missed the deadline to nominate a staff member who has made a difference in my experience here at UMKC, but Dr. Lori Reesor has made such a positive impact on my experience here that it would be robbery not to include her in the recognition.

I am a single parent who has had to overcome many obstacles on my journey for the attainment of higher education. There were many times that Dr. Reesor could have given up on me as a student and made the decision not to admit me, which would have been a devastating blow to my life, but she believed in me and worked diligently with me to come to a solution that absolutely worked out for the best for me. She has been patient and trusted my abilities, and that has made all of the difference in my life as well as my children, as I do not have long before I will graduate with my master's in education, curriculum and instruction. Dr. Reesor believed in me, which helped me further believe in myself, and I am hoping that you take into consideration all that she has done to help me make a better life for myself and my children.

I know that deadlines are important, but I did not have access to a computer from home, and when I came to campus in the evenings, I never had the opportunity to visit a table where I could nominate her because I have to work during the day. Dr. Reesor definitely deserves recognition, and I hope that she is not slighted because I was slow on the draw.

Thank you in advance for understanding my plight and recognizing the most awesome dean employed at UMKC.

Sincerely,
Jennifer Brothers (pseudonym)

Tears welled into my eyes as I read Jennifer's letter. She was a student whom I had frequently talked with on the telephone but had met only once or twice in person. She was a bright and articulate student but had experienced a number of difficulties and tragedies throughout her life. Thinking back to the time I spent working with Jennifer, I remembered her as a strong woman who didn't show much emotion. She was a fighter, and I could tell she had fought for most of the successes in her life. I remember spending time with her on the phone, trying to help her figure out how to keep her life on track and finish her degree. Although our interactions were challenging at times, I respected her as an individual and wanted to help her succeed.

At the luncheon, students had the option of sharing their stories about their nominee, and Jennifer spoke about me. Again I was deeply touched. Jennifer demonstrated her ability to speak thoughtfully and eloquently. She even knew I had just had a baby and expressed her good wishes to me. She was so kind and thoughtful in her presentation. I never had imagined I had this much impact on Jennifer, or that she was that appreciative. That she took the time to write this nomination and participate in the luncheon meant so much to me.

I found Jennifer after the luncheon, thanked her, and reached out to hug her. She stepped back, cautious and hesitant, but eventually let me hug her. Then she quickly left the room. I thought maybe through this event we had formed a new bond and that we would stay connected, but that's not what Jennifer wanted. Although we have not stayed in contact, Jennifer remains my constant reminder that every phone call, e-mail request, appeal form, and student contact can make a difference in someone's life. My goal every day is to always listen to students closely and carefully, treat them with the respect they deserve, and do my best to help them attain their educational goals. That's the difference Jennifer has made in my career, and I will always be grateful to her.

ORIENT ME
BY
MONICA PARIKH

"Was I making a big mistake? What does an engineer actually do? Five years of classes and co-ops? A male-to-female ratio of 16 to 1? But everyone was so proud of me. How could I turn down a scholarship to Rochester Institut of Technology (RIT)?"

My introduction to the next five years was a three-day summer orientation. My parents drove me to RIT. My mother was cool and composed, offering a loving care-package for my stay and excellent advice for my future. My father, however, was visibly nervous. Maybe it hadn't hit him that his little girl would be leaving. Maybe he doubted my capacity to handle the rigorous coursework. Maybe he was recalling how media portrays college—parties, drugs, sex. Maybe it was everything bombarding him at once—his coffee was too cold, the car was too hot, the campus was too hard to find, my bag was too heavy.

When we arrived at the campus, my optimistic anticipation of my first weekend at college was quenched by apprehension. I was scared that one more thing would upset my father. I feared the proverbial "last straw." We pulled into the parking lot, and a cheerful girl in short-shorts rollerbladed over to our car. "She doesn't look like an engineer," I thought. As it turns out, she wasn't. She was an industrial design major and a tennis player. "They have sports here?" I asked, exposing I had done far too little research during the college application process. She answered my questions and chit-chatted with us, explaining why it was taking so long for the line of cars to reach the door.

I saw other parents laughing with their kids—fathers giving sons the "atta boy" treatment and mothers double-checking that their daughters' lava lamps hadn't tipped. In my car, the tension could be cut with a knife. Over came another parking-lot staffer to soothe my father. I thought, "Better send in the troops... two ain't gonna do it." But it did. This pair of college kids changed our tune. They gave us a clear explanation of the congestion and candid thoughts on the weekend schedule. They spoke of placement exams, swimming pools, job fairs, balloon blowing, academic advising, and ice cream socials. They offered their take on courses, the city, residence life, tutors, food, and faculty. They stayed by our side as the cars crawled toward the entrance, completely committed to our happiness. I have never been better served. These orientation angels changed my negative perception. They infused us with energy and optimism, shifting my gears from dreading each moment to actively engaging in a rewarding orientation.

"Who were they?' I asked myself.

A few weeks after classes started, I went to the orientation office. I didn't know who those two heaven-sent students were or why it was their duty to stand in 90-degree heat and cheer up parents, but someone deserved some credit. I didn't know how to phrase it, so I simply said, "I want to thank you guys for helping my family make a tough transition this summer." The secretary coldly told me, "We're not hiring." I explained that she had misunderstood me. I really just wanted to thank them for having students in the parking lots because incoming parents are even more scared than incoming students. Apparently I'm loud, because the director of orientation heard me. She took me into her office and explained that there is a division of labor between administration and students who execute orientation. Administrators plan and fund, and the students volunteer to do everything else. "Are you kidding me?" I said, astonished. "They were volunteers?" I burst out crying.

I thought, "How could all those students be volunteers, in that heat with parents complaining and students repeating the same questions and people threatening to sue and car exhaust and...it was their summer vacation!"

"What wonderful students," I sobbed. Trying to console me, she offered me an application to join the Student Orientation Services volunteer leaders. I applied and was warmly received. The next two years, I willingly worked harder than expected, recruiting other volunteers, giving tours, managing signage, soothing parents, fetching breakfast, convincing students of the importance of academic advising, and getting students involved on campus. My involvement with student affairs benefited me infinitely. It taught me the value of a holistic education. I learned by practice that an involved student fared well—greater satisfaction and better retention. I was hooked and decided to make this my career.

To better understand how a university serves its students, I decided to pursue a master's degree in higher education administration. After I enrolled, my advisor recommended, "Get an internship this summer." I knew just where to go. I called RIT and volunteered again, but this time I was going to serve in a completely different capacity. Instead of being the student appeasing new arrivals in a hot parking lot, I was the administrator on the phone, making reservations, mapping logistics, updating the Web site, training volunteers, and securing funding. It was the best summer of my life. I worked 16-hour days to thank the students who worked that 16-hour day for me. Student affairs came full-circle.

RUNNING ON PAVEMENT

BY

GYPSY M. DENZINE

It has been well over a decade since I met Trevor. He was an 18-year-old first-year student who taught me two important lessons. As soon as I met him on opening day in the residence halls, I knew that he was a runner. His build, the type of running shoes he wore, and the runner's watch on his wrist were clear signs. In fact, I could tell by his appearance that he was probably a middle-distance runner. For many years, I have been around collegiate track and field and cross-country. I have enjoyed timing at meets, working with intercollegiate athletic tutoring programs, and doing volunteer recruiting when I can. When I saw Trevor in line waiting to get his room key, I said, "Welcome to Upper Midwest Polytechnic College [UMPC, a fictitious name]. You must be a runner." He smiled and said, "Yes, ma'am. I'm an 800-meter runner." We talked about running for a while, and I encouraged him to let me know how he was doing.

I saw Trevor about two weeks after the semester started and asked him how he was doing. He said overall things were fine. His classes were going well, but he was not used to running on pavement. Trevor moved to the "big city" to attend UMPC. The school had an enrollment of approximately 10,000 undergraduate students and was located in a town with a population of 50,000. Trevor grew up in a small rural town about 400 miles away from the campus. His family lived on a ranch, and it was a 2.5-mile run on a dirt road from his house to the end of his driveway. On days when he did "double runs," his short run was to the end of his driveway and back. In addition to having to adjust to running on pavement, he told me he was not used to going for a run and having to stop at stoplights. Trevor also told me his high school graduating class had 28 students, 17 of them male. He now shared a community bathroom in his residence hall with more guys than that. In high school, it took him 45 minutes to get to school by car, so it amazed him that he could roll out of bed in his room at UMPC and be in class 10 minutes later.

I had arrived at UMPC about three weeks prior to Trevor. In contrast to his experience, I relocated after living in a large city and working at a large urban campus. As a runner, I was thrilled that I could run on the UMPC campus and not have to fight city traffic and breathe smog. It had been years since I had run on anything but pavement. I was enjoying my new position in residence life at UMPC and knew that I had made a good decision in leaving my previous job. In mid-October, I received an incident report from one of the resident assistants saying that over the weekend she had seen Trevor in the hallway of his residence hall with a full bottle of beer in his hand. I sent Trevor a letter, asking him to schedule a time for us to discuss his alleged violation. After receiving my letter, he called immediately to schedule an appointment. The Friday morning we were to meet, something came up, and I called Trevor to reschedule. We agreed to meet on Monday morning.

When Trevor came to my office, he looked very nervous. I began our discussion with an explanation of the purpose of our meeting. I included some informal remarks because he looked so nervous. I asked him about his classes and his running, both of which were going fine. He was getting accustomed to sharing a bathroom with other students, and, although it was difficult, he was adjusting to running on pavement. When I noticed he still looked quite anxious, I asked him if he was OK. He said he had barely slept the entire weekend. He confirmed that he did, in fact, have a beer in the hallway, and he knew it was a mistake. He assumed he would lose his track scholarship and would have to drop out of school. He was upset because he did not know how he would tell his parents, and his family could not afford to pay for college. He was the first in his family to go to college.

During our meeting, Trevor told me that he assumed I rescheduled our Friday meeting to make him "sweat it out" over the weekend. He looked tired, and he was on the verge of tears. Finding him responsible for violating the alcohol policy, I informed him that he would be placed on probation for the remainder of the academic year. I explained probation and cautioned him against further violations, and noted that he could stay in school and would not lose his track scholarship. In addition, I said I would not share any information about this incident with his track coach.

He then said to me, "But now comes the hard part. I have to tell my parents." I told Trevor I would not send his parents a copy of the probation letter. I explained that even if his parents contacted me, I could not discuss matters related to this situation. Trevor responded, "I have to tell them." Thinking he misunderstood me, I repeated that I would not say anything to his parents. Reinforcing the point, I said, "The only way they will find out is if you tell them." Trevor said to me, "It's not about them finding out. My parents would want to know. This has been really hard for me, and my parents would want to know that I am going through a difficult time but that I will be OK."

Let me return to the two important lessons I learned from this situation with Trevor. First, to this day, I cannot remember what came up that led me to reschedule my original Friday appointment with Trevor. Things do come up and I still need to reschedule meetings with students on occasion. However, I am much more sensitive today when I reschedule meetings. I have never believed in a "make them sweat it out" philosophy. The second lesson I learned from Trevor was an important one about college student development and the balance between autonomy and intimacy. What I initially perceived to be a lack of autonomy on Trevor's part turned out to be a positive example of a young man's ability to maintain close and mature relationships with his family.

Trevor graduated from UMPC and returned to his hometown to live and work. I do not know if he is still running. I moved to a new university and town that have a wonderful dirt urban trail system. I no longer run on pavement. There are still times when I am running on the dirt trail that I think about Trevor. He taught me important lessons about respecting students and being aware of my own biases when meeting with them.

FOR THE LOVE OF J-SKI
BY
WILLIAM B. BYNUM JR.

As a young college student who came from a small town and an impoverished, single-parent household of eight, I was fortunate enough, given my academic and athletic prowess, to attend one of the nation's top 10 national liberal arts colleges. I heard often from my teachers, coaches, and principals that I chose an excellent college and that my future career prospects would be ensured. As a young man from a low-income family, I studied, worked, and played with fellow students who came from upper- and upper-middle-class households and had attended prep schools. My classmates had possessions beyond my wildest imagination and had traveled the United States and the world prior to college. While my academic knowledge was as good, my knowledge of other things was extremely small in comparison. Born and raised in North Carolina, I had traveled outside the state only twice, taking car trips to Philadelphia and Washington, D.C.

As I got to know my classmates, I learned about their lives and travels. I promised myself that I too would avail myself of the wonders of the United States when I had the opportunity. I was a good student academically and was active on campus, serving as captain of the football team, president of the Black Student Coalition, and a campus disc jockey; acting in leading roles in three campus plays; and serving on several presidential and dean advisory committees. While I enjoyed my college experience, upon graduation I recommitted myself to the promise that I would travel every chance I got. I also decided to include my nephews so that when they entered college, they could be active participants in discussions about the wonders of our country.

I kept this promise to my nephews and myself. Each summer and during certain holidays, my nephews and I traveled. To name a few destinations, we visited New York City; Virginia Beach, Va.; Myrtle Beach, S.C.; Hilton Head, S.C.; Atlanta; Orlando, Fla., and Disney World; Panama City, Fla.; and Charleston, S.C. My nephews and their parents thanked me immensely for providing this experience. I continued to expose my nephews to travel and college life once I began my higher education career. They quickly fell in love with the colleges I served and their beautiful campuses. Three of the four nephews who experienced these summer and holiday trips—Raphael, Jonathan (J-Ski) and Christopher (C-Money)—chose to attend historically black colleges. The nicknames in parentheses were the ones I gave them during our summers together. My nephews told me how important these trips were, how they felt comfortable discussing travel with their college classmates, and how they had traveled more extensively than most of their peers.

When it was time to choose a college, Jonathan and Christopher decided to attend the college where I was the associate vice president. Because they spent their high school summers with me, they were familiar with the campus and my colleagues.

Jonathan (J-Ski) was a slim, handsome, somewhat shy and reserved young man but had a good sense of humor and love of life. He listened well and was a friend to all. He was the type of young man for whom college was designed. I focus on Jonathan because he was the type of young man who truly benefited from what college had to offer and why I continue to love my chosen profession. Jonathan loved college life. He served on his freshman hall council and visited my colleagues in their offices. He was extremely respectful and always a nice guy. I would see this likable young man around campus, giving hugs and hand-shakes to students and staff. He entered college as a shy, laid-back young man; with each year he became more confident, more well-rounded, more worldly and mature, yet he maintained his respectfulness, morals, and values. I watched with great pride and joy his maturity, growth, and development.

While I was on medical leave during the spring semester of Jonathan's junior year, I received the worst phone call of my life. My secretary informed me that on the morning of April 18, Jonathan had passed away. He was suffering from an irregular heartbeat. He went to a local medical center, where the physician simply prescribed a medicine for patients with severe heart conditions rather than run further tests or prolong his observation. The medication was too strong, and he suffered a heart attack in his sleep. This tragedy hit my family and the campus community hard. His mother and father later received a malpractice settlement from the HMO and doctor, but it in no way comes anywhere close to healing the loss that they and Jonathan's other family and friends have suffered. We all continue to miss him.

The days following J-Ski's death were the hardest of my life. The pain, the loss, the questioning of God, and the bereavement of family and friends were almost overwhelming. I leaned heavily on my faith, and I followed the awesome example of his mom and dad. Given these two factors, I managed to be a pillar of strength for our family given the most tragic loss and most difficult time we ever faced. His mom and dad asked that I speak at his memorial service. Rather than mourning his death, we celebrated his life.

Upon returning to work from medical leave, I found the campus full of memories of J-Ski and our times together. The memories were too real and numerous. As a result, I decided to take an opportunity at another historically black college. I continue to love what I do for a living and wake up each and every day excited to go to work because of my memory of J-Ski and how much the college experience can develop young people and help them become the persons they desire to be.

I continue to see J-Ski every day in the faces, lives, and experiences of the students I come in contact with and have the opportunity to influence. I take my job seriously, and I know the impact that my example, actions, attitudes, and interactions have on our young. I feel great pride and joy as I welcome students each year. I see J-Skis everywhere, in young men and women, in blacks and whites. Since his passing, I don't recall ever having "a bad day." I've had days that I once would have called "bad," but given my love and belief in God and my love for Jonathan and his parents, I always see a silver lining. I work tirelessly to make sure that the decisions I make, the people I lead, and the manner in which I interact with students, faculty, and staff are positive.

I dedicate the remainder of my days on this earth and the inspiration I help provide for those seeking a higher education to the love and memory of J-Ski, Jonathan Lamar Boone.

THE IDLERS OF THE BAMBOO GROVE
BY
JAY R. COOPER

Like many others, I entered the student affairs profession rather precariously because of my involvement as an undergraduate student. My initial activities outside of the classroom included a brief stint in the resident housing association, involvement in the student program board and student government, and even being a member of "Nader's Raiders" public interest research group. While each of these experiences contributed to my entry into the field, it was another, more profound experience that crystallized my decision to enter student affairs.During my junior year, several suitemates and I hatched a plan to register a student organization that would challenge not only the office of student activities but the institutional culture. We also wondered whether we could get funding from student government for the silliest idea we could conceive.

Our conversations led to the creation of an organization with the auspicious title of the Fiber Optic Byberphone Society (FOBS). To this day, I am not sure what a Byberphone is, but I know that it originated with Monty Python's Flying Circus. Obviously, FOBS did not take hold. Our conversations continued into the night until one of my suitemates began talking about his East Asian studies course and the class discussions about a seventh-century Chinese philosopher named Li Po. Li Po, according to this student, founded a group of radical thinkers who called themselves the Six Idlers of the Bamboo Grove. Their mission was to drink wine and write poetry. "That's it," we all exclaimed in unison. We serendipitously found a mission, a purpose, and a title. We would become the twentieth-century version of the Six Idlers of the Bamboo Grove. While none of us claimed to be poets, we did enjoy wine and figured we could attempt to tap into our creative potential.

All of the appropriate paperwork was collected and submitted. We filled out the required sections of the student organization approval forms with the intent of challenging the administration. Rather than having the traditional officer positions of president and vice president, we opted for captain and first mates. Our constitution was modeled after the Communist Manifesto. We found an unsuspecting faculty advisor in the English department (the Honors College, no less). To this day, I'm sure that our faculty advisor was never fully aware of our group's activities. Within several weeks, we received word that the Idlers of the Bamboo Grove was approved, no questions asked. We felt great satisfaction in having weathered the campus bureaucracy.

In the spirit of Li Po, our first meeting would be held off-campus at a local watering hole, the Hog's Breath Inn. We began as a fairly small, loosely knit group, who in many ways represented the full spectrum of the student body. Over the course of the next several weeks, through word of mouth, the group quickly grew to 20 to 30 students each week. We befriended the owner of the Hog's Breath Inn as well as the regulars who drove trucks for the local Pepsi Cola bottling plant. They became our comrades, although baffled by our group's activities. We shared a community space, yet each brought unique perspectives and contexts to the environment of the Hog's Breath Inn. All of us, no doubt, considered ourselves nontraditional students, not in terms of our ages but rather our perceived status as outsiders. We all had deep interests in culture, music, and art but had not found a home for these interests on campus. We created a milieu off-campus where we could celebrate these interests.

Meetings were an opportunity to unleash our creative potential through spontaneous writing. None of us had any real training or aspirations in creative writing. We decided as a group to let the evenings and the ideas unfold. At the end of each "meeting," various scraps of paper and cocktail napkins were collected on which the Idlers wrote their musings. These were stuffed into a folder, which grew in size over time.

Some used pseudonyms: W.D. Deadman, Yolanda the Cat Woman, Jack Magnum, The Lonely Women, Johnny Earwig, and Attikiss Juice. Others bared their souls by attaching their names to their writing and publishing it for public inspection.

Over a semester of writing and pitchers of Stroh's beer, we talked world events, politics, literature, music, and pop culture. The Reagan era had begun, and there was a great deal to discuss and debate. We shared our perspectives with each other and claimed our own liberal arts education.

Within several months, we collected bits of interesting poetry, short stories, satire, and illustrations. Some of the writing had moments of clarity and near brilliance, while others were mere ramblings but were still given our full attention for the hidden meanings that may have lain between the lines. Collaborative writing efforts were not uncommon. Everything at an Idlers meeting was considered "art."

Our next challenge became what to do with all that we had written. We also still had our unrealized goal of securing funding from student government. It was agreed that we would submit a request to have our musings published and distributed across campus. To our surprise, student government approved the request, and we were off to the campus print shop to figure out how to put the whole mess together. We developed a cover, wrote a preface and acknowledgments, learned about printing, copyrighting, and distribution. We deliberated and argued, resolved conflicts, and learned new perspectives. Along the way, we also learned about leadership and collaboration, and developed more mature interpersonal relationships.

The organization continued to grow in terms of the number of students and in its notoriety. Six volumes of poetry were published, involving nearly 300 students. The local city paper featured a story on our activities. As a campus fundraiser, we printed T-shirts with our logo. The university gave us an office. At year's end, the student activities office gave us the Low Budget Program Award. We couldn't believe that a motley group of students, who challenged the rules and the status quo, could gain any campus recognition.

In time, we all graduated and moved on to the important tasks of the "real world." Many of my friends from the Idlers of the Bamboo Grove still stay in contact; others have moved on, never to be heard from again. The Hog's Breath Inn is now a CVS pharmacy, but our legacy lives on in our minds and in the archives of the university library. I met my wife while we both were Idlers, as well as my best friend and future best man. Some of us married, and some have since divorced. What remains are the memories of a truly powerful undergraduate experience and education.

While I benefited greatly from my experiences in other student affairs programs and academic experiences, I developed most profoundly during my two years as an Idler of the Bamboo Grove. I made the shift from adolescence to young adulthood because of the interaction with my peers. It also instilled in me my commitment to campus involvement, to the concept of student development and student affairs, to the creative process, to challenging institutional and social norms, and to finding opportunities for others who may feel like they are "on the fringes" to become involved on campus.

In many ways, the Idlers remind me of the early literary societies in American higher education. We met off-campus, not necessarily in secret but on our own terms. We celebrated our own way of living and immersed ourselves in our passions and interests. We grew and developed together. While there were many in student affairs who challenged and supported what we were doing as a student organization and were influential in the success of the group, their hands-off approach was what was needed for that organization at that time. We must not lose sight of the fact that student development can and does occur in those spaces on campus, that we do not need to "manage" every aspect of students' lives outside of the classroom. In our case, lives were changed as a result of some late-night conversations among friends and a little poetry-in-action.

The earth is my bed and the sky is my blanket. -Li Po

MY BEGINNING
BY
KATY VENCE

The request was a simple task from a dear friend and former hall director: Write a composition about my experiences in residence life. It didn't seem too challenging or outrageous, until I sat down to say what needed to be said. That's when I lost my words.

I haven't always been the woman I am today, but reflecting back, it is often difficult to see myself in any other place. I was not always the person who writes now, from the Peace Corps office computer in Pretoria, South Africa, my brown hair streaked blond, my face pink and freckled from the scourging sun. I haven't always been here on this African soil, speaking words of the Tswana people and living the life of a volunteer.

Let me lead you down the path I followed to arrive at this destination, a wayward village so far away from home. Based on the paths I've taken, I can see that my life was meant to follow this particular calling. It wasn't merely coincidence. It started when I first saw that resident advisor flyer during my freshman year. Who would have imagined it would mark my beginning?

At the time I saw the flyer, I didn't know what I was doing. I have always been a person to speak with conviction and passion, but at that point in my life, I really didn't know what I was saying or doing. Truthfully, I was lost. A freshman in a crowd of 18,000 students, I could not decide if I was trying to fit in or trying to stand out. I come from a small town in Ohio, so it was easy to follow the rest. College had the potential to offer the same flow—I could have easily blended in. Although I arrived on campus green, by the second semester I convinced myself that I had life figured out. College was becoming everything I expected it to be, but something crucial was missing. I was going through the motions with very little action or reaction. I was floating, instead of soaring as I had hoped. A void needed to be filled, and I was becoming desperate to fill it.

It was a simple moment that turned me from the meaningless road I was traveling to the victorious path I base my life on now. I recall pausing at that resident advisor flyer on my walk home from class. I did just as the flyer recommended, followed my heart, and applied to be a resident advisor. I endured the grueling application process and participated in interview after interview, closed-down scenarios, and group discussions. I was not confident or proud of my performances that day, but I hoped that the decision-makers saw something in me that set me apart from the rest.

I was sitting on my futon in my little room when I received the phone call. I couldn't believe it! My luck was finally changing! Not only was I offered an R.A. position for the following school year, I was asked to begin immediately. I hung up the phone, baffled by the proposal and anxious about the lifestyle changes. Did I really want to venture into a whole new world so soon? Was I ready for this next step? After a few days of serious contemplation and many reservations, I agreed to accept the R.A. position.

I began my position after spring break my freshman year. I wish I could tell you that I fit in right away with the staff members and the residents on my floor. The staff was not accustomed to my inexperienced presence, and the women on my floor were unwilling to yield to my timid approach to loud hip-hop music and obnoxious voices. My certainty faltered, as did my steady grade-point average. I began to doubt my ability to be great but signed up for another year of resident advising with the hope that things would work out.

After a suffocating summer in my parents' home with my three brothers, and working the early-morning shift at the local bakery, I returned to school early for R.A. training. My second experience as an R.A. left much to be desired. My floor of 45 freshman women terrorized me with silly pranks and offensive gestures. They did everything from scratching curse words into my door to spraying shaving cream over the shower stall. They cussed me out to my face and littered the hallway with toilet paper and broken broomsticks.

Enough was enough. I was at my wits' end. I could see that the timid girl I was the year before had to grow up quickly. I tried to maintain my peaceful disposition, but the residents were bringing me to the edge of my sanity. I had no choice but to lay down the law.

My hall director, who became my mentor and good friend, believed in my ability to rise above. At the end of the school year, I sat with him, thankful I had survived but uncertain I could withstand another year of abuse and defeat. He heard my ramblings, weak excuses, and lame confessions. The one question he asked me that I still consider today was, "Have you learned all you can from this experience?" The answer was a simple, definite "No."

When my third chance as an R.A. approached, I was more confident than ever. That year was more successful than the previous one, something I attribute to my fresh hardened attitude and open-eyed perspective. The women on the floor respected me because I learned to insist upon it. In anticipation of my hall director's departing question, I was determined to learn as much as possible from this experience. I was ready.

Sometime during that year, my hall director asked the resident advisors to list our individual life goals. Before then, I had far-fetched ideas and lofty dreams but hadn't written them down or actually spoken them. I was a stronger woman than I was three years earlier, but I was still easily influenced by others' opinions of me. When forced to examine my little list, I began to feel more confident. Who said I couldn't accomplish these dreams? Who said I had to live my life according to other people's perceptions of me? I liked how these ambitions looked on paper and rolled off my tongue with conviction. The most demanding of all my dreams was joining the Peace Corps, so I began there.

As a Peace Corps volunteer living and working in this desolate South African village among people who speak a different language and live according to different rules, I am often alone with my thoughts. My solitude always brings me back to my resident advisor days, and sometimes I can even draw parallels to that life and the one I live today. I was challenged there like I constantly am here. I lived my life in a tiny fishbowl as an R.A., and I live with an audience at my doorstep here. Whether I am comfortable with it or not, I have served both communities as a role model. My life as an R.A. has prepared me for my life as a Peace Corps volunteer. It gave me the tools I needed to survive with the conviction and faith I always wanted to live by.

Even an ocean away, I remain in close contact with my hall director and fellow resident advisors. They continue to be a solid part of my unwavering support system. When everyone thought I wasn't strong enough for two years of service in a small African village, these people stood by my side, encouraging me every step of the way. From this distance, it is simple to reflect on my life and the roads I have taken. Nothing will ever replace in my heart the years I spent as a resident advisor and the people I met throughout my journey. For that and for the courageous woman I have become because of that one flyer advertising an R.A.'s life, I will forever be grateful.

STORIES FROM THE FRONT:
A COLLECTION OF STUDENT SERVICES ANECDOTES
BY
KEVIN POLLOCK

Those who have chosen a career in student services and student affairs will gladly tell you that their lives are enriched because of the numerous positive interactions with students and the knowledge that they are making a difference in so many lives. The caring individuals in student services have heard students' tales, occasionally heart-wrenching ones detailing family strife, financial difficulties, and educational problems. On the flip side, student services employees are also privy to another set of stories. Every now and then, these stories emerge detailing interactions with students that bring a smile, laugh, or gentle reminder of the humor that also can be found in our work.

A quick call to friends in the profession brought the following humorous stories of students:

> An irate student at one college left a message on the financial aid answering machine telling them to correct the spelling of his name. Unfortunately, he didn't leave a name.

> One student hand-carried a grade change over to the registrar's office (a definite no-no). There was reason to suspect that it had been altered by the student from a WF (withdraw failing) to a WP (withdraw passing). The WF was in blue ink. The addition to make it a P was in red ink.

> A counselor from an engineering college suggested to the student with whom he was working that he should perhaps contact another engineering college, Lawrence Tech. The student then asked if he could have Larry's phone number.

> A female counselor described in detail the phone conversation she had with a prospective male student who went to the bathroom during the phone call. The counselor could hear every detail of the trip to the restroom, including the flush.

> Another counselor received an "urgent" phone call from a student who then fell asleep on the phone during the counselor's response.

> During a phone campaign to alumni, a student found out that the

person he was trying to reach had passed away. After trying three times to write the word "deceased" on the contact sheet, he finally gave up in exasperation and wrote, "He's dead."

A financial aid office sent a student a form which required a spouse's signature. The student retuned the form and had written in the spouse's signature space, "diseased." The office interpreted that to mean deceased.

A newly enrolled student walked into one student services office to inquire where he could obtain a hall pass.

One financial aid office received a phone call from an individual asking if she had to be a student to receive financial aid.

A student asked one counselor, "If I register for an online class, do I have to have a computer?"

In one business office, a student called the cashier and inquired if his tuition payment had been received. The cashier indicated that no payment was showing on his account. She asked, "Where did you mail it from?" The student responded, "My mailbox."

One student complained to a counselor about all the reading he had to do for an online class.

Finally, one counselor recalled a student who called him several years ago and said he wanted to be an anti-theseologist. The counselor talked about the training needed to become an anesthesiologist, but the student insisted that he wanted to be an anti-theseologist. The counselor then told him that to be an anesthesiologist, he would need to complete medical school and then specialize in that area. The student gave it some thought and decided to not pursue the field of anti-theseology. The moral of the story: If you can't pronounce the profession, you can't do the job.

Of course, we realize that out there somewhere are students who are telling the same types of stories about their interactions with staff members in the student services offices.

THE DAY I WAS JEALOUS OF JESUS

BY

JAMES RHATIGAN

One day, I was crossing the campus for a meeting. I was running late and was somewhat preoccupied, often the case for people in student affairs. Walking in the opposite direction was a crying student, obviously experiencing considerable stress. After a few steps, I decided the meeting could wait and turned around to catch the woman. I gave her my card, told her I noticed she was upset, and asked if there was anything I could do to help.

The woman sobbed and told me she had just discovered that her husband had left her. He told her he had fallen in love with someone else. On top of that, he had withdrawn the money from their meager checking account, leaving her with virtually nothing. She said she had two children and therefore no choice but to drop out of school and find a job. I learned that she was a junior. Certain that some way could be found to keep her in school, I persuaded her to walk with me to my office.

When we arrived, I presented her with some alternatives. I provided an immediate $300 grant from a donor who had told me to use it as I saw fit. I explained the possibilities of a long-term loan and arranged for her to meet with a financial aid officer. I mentioned that occasionally it was helpful for people to consult with a counselor when they were under stress. I explained that her student fees covered the costs of counseling and gave her two names to call. More important, I was able to get a solid lead for a half-time campus job. Everything fell into place, and I felt good about her chances of overcoming this very difficult circumstance.

When I was finished, I asked if there was anything else she could think of that we needed to do at that moment. She answered by averting her eyes, looking at her folded hands in her lap, and softly saying, "I just want to say, thank you, Jesus." I almost blurted out loud, "Jesus! What did Jesus have to do with this?" Then the truth revealed itself. Helping the woman was not enough. I also wanted the credit. I call that memorable day the "Day I Was Jealous of Jesus." We should not avoid acknowledging our personal shortcomings and foibles. We can be helpful in spite of them.

A LIFE REMEMBERED, A LIFE TRANSFORMED

BY

MINDY MICHELS

In memory of and with profound gratitude to Wanda Alston.

My friend died on Wednesday. It wasn't an expected death or even a death from which you can somehow find a way to give meaning. She was senselessly murdered by a drug-crazed neighbor in the middle of the day while she was in her home. I found out from the news on Thursday morning because my friend was a member of the mayor's cabinet in the District of Columbia and the acting director of the city's Office of Lesbian, Gay, Bisexual, and Transgender Affairs. In the days since Wanda died, I've spent time thinking about her life and the contributions she made to the city, to gay, lesbian, bisexual, and transgender communities, to communities of color, and to the people who knew her.

Everyone I talked to was devastated by the loss of a woman who has been described as tenacious, energetic, passionate, and feisty. She was a vital figure in the development of the District's black gay community and had a role in both local and national organizing. Her acute political skills helped shape Washington, D.C. She never backed down, demanding that our city include gay people and that the gay community include all of our diversity. She inspired me with her fierce commitment. And now she's gone.

Since her death was announced, I've received calls from friends and acquaintances wanting to talk about her, wanting to understand how this could have happened. Often the calls have blended into one another, with everyone feeling the same grief, confusion, and anger. But one call today stood out from the rest.

I answered the phone, and the caller was a former student named Ahmed. Four years ago, he spent a semester attending the university where I worked. He was an international student from Pakistan who found the freedom and support to come out as a gay man while he was studying in the United States. He graduated, moved to the D.C. area, and stayed in touch while he looked for a job. After a few months, he was running short on time left on his visa without any prospects of a position that would allow him to remain in the United States. He was afraid of the potential consequences of going home to Pakistan. I was one of the people he called as he anxiously searched for possible connections that might lead to a job or internship. While I was not hopeful that I could help him, I told him to send me his résumé and I would see what I could do. The next evening, I happened to have dinner with Wanda and her partner. Given that Wanda was well-connected in the District government, I mentioned Ahmed to her and she asked me to send along his résumé. Within days, Ahmed had an interview for an internship with the director of a D.C. government agency. Nearly two years later, he is still working there in a full-time position and attending a graduate program to earn a master's in public health.

Ahmed called because he saw the news about Wanda's murder. He was concerned about me and called to find out how I was doing and to express his sadness about her death. Though I had spent the better part of the previous two days thinking about Wanda, until I spoke to him I had forgotten about her role in helping him years earlier. Ahmed thanked me profusely for assisting him in finding a job. He told me how much he loved his work and how grateful he was to still be in the United States. Over and over, in numerous phone calls, he has told me that he could not fully express his appreciation to Wanda and me.

Today his gratitude took on a whole new meaning. Like all of us, I enjoy being able to help students. I derive pleasure and passion from my work directing the Gay, Lesbian, Bisexual, Transgender and Ally Resource Center at American University because sometimes I can see the impact the office has on the lives of the students who walk through our doors. Ahmed is not the first student that I have helped find an internship, though he is probably the one who needed it the most. He is also not the only student I have watched transform and grow into a self-assured professional, perhaps in some small part due to our interactions.

What was different today was that in calling me, Ahmed evoked what is truly important. Not only did Ahmed remind me that I made a difference in his life, he reminded me of Wanda's commitment to others and her willingness to always extend a hand to help someone else. Wanda's gesture on Ahmed's behalf only took her a moment but was based on the foundation of her years of dedication, hard work, and activism. In that moment, she and I enduringly altered the course of Ahmed's life.

I will never again walk into a room and watch Wanda direct the action. I will never go to another rally and see her speak. I will never have another dinner with her and her partner. I will never again call her when a student can use a helping hand. Her life reminds me that all of our actions make a difference, some of them with lasting impact. We make a difference in other people's lives not only because of what we do but because of who we are in relation to one another. Ahmed's short call spoke volumes to me about the importance of our interconnectedness: Ahmed to me, me to Wanda, and back again. While nothing will ever bring Wanda back, nothing will ever erase her either—not from my life, not from Ahmed's life, not from the lives of the countless other people whom she touched.

THE WOMEN'S CENTER MADE A MAN OUT OF ME

BY
HEATH HUBER

"I thank God that I'm not a woman, but sometimes I wish I wasn't a man." This verse from an old song has special meaning for me as I reflect on my career in student affairs. As an undergraduate student, I never paid much attention to feminist issues, and I rarely took violence against women seriously.

Participation in a sexual assault prevention program in graduate school quickly changed my attitude. I became seriously concerned with issues of violence against women and developed a passion for advocating for women's issues. Eventually, I even took a position as a male educator at a university's women's center. Following years of joking about feminism and being ignorant about it, I was suddenly willingly enmeshed in it, informed by it, and advocating it as a way to prevent gender violence. In retrospect, even though I was the educator, it turns out that I was the one who was really learning. My instructors were the many women and men I met through the Women's Center who shared a common interest in stopping gender-based violence. One survivor in particular taught me about strength, courage, and the importance of my work.

Before I go on, I have to admit that it is a tough time to be a man. As various voices critique society, some men feel like they are being blamed for every evil in the world today. I know I felt blamed. Often when I present on gender violence to classes and organizations, I look at the faces of the male students and see myself when I was in their position. I see their anger and frustration as they struggle to develop their identities, yet feel bombarded with what they see as anti-male messages when it comes to sexual assault and domestic violence.

Talk about "touchy" issues. Try talking to men about issues of sexual assault, violence, and especially about masculinity. Men are so invested in what it is to "be a man" that when you talk about concepts like masculinity and violence, they get very defensive. I have spent a long time educating others about violence and masculinity, and the reception I receive varies from pro-feminists to promise keepers. Everyone has an idea of what it means to "be a man." I have to confess, I am no exception. All my life I wanted to be more of "a man," whatever that means. I have never been able to live up to the model. I am awful at sports. I choose not to drink alcohol. I walk away from fights. I worked at a women's center, and I care about preventing violence. I found I couldn't fit the "masculine mold." Sometimes I felt as if, with all the lessons I had taught on responsible masculinity, I never learned what being "a man" really meant.

That lesson came, however, when my job ended. After four years, the grant that funded our whole victim advocacy program and my position as an educator was not renewed. Our program was finished. The education I offered and the direct crisis intervention that our victim advocates provided would be gone. I had to face the reality that everything we had worked for was over.

Out of this tragedy, though, came rays of hope as the students stepped in to try to save us. There were letter-writing campaigns, fundraisers, and meetings with senior-level administrators. It was inspiring to watch our students advocate for what they valued and to see how these values shaped their decisions, choices, and actions. Among these students was Robin.

After her first year of college, Robin was drugged and raped by three men. The experience was humiliating, terrifying, and devastating. She took that pain, however, and turned it into action. She joined our campus sexual assault prevention organization, took every opportunity to get involved in violence issues, and eventually spoke publicly about her experience to help raise awareness and educate others. Her enthusiasm, courage, and ability to answer tough questions amazed me. It was an honor to facilitate presentations with her and support her efforts.

Because of our frequent interactions in programming, she eventually asked me to help her prepare for what was to be her first public presentation about her assault. She wanted to integrate some of the journal entries she wrote about her experience into her presentation. She asked me to read her journal to help her determine the appropriate excerpts. As I sat at my desk reading her innermost thoughts about the assault and its aftermath, I realized the kind of trust she was giving me. I felt blessed and unworthy all at once. Her last entry had a profound effect on me because it detailed how her experience led her to distrust and hate men in general. She wrote, "I think one of the hardest parts of recovery is when you're to the point where you have begun to forgive the opposite sex." She expressed having difficulty finding it in her heart to forgive.

I was having a difficult time too. I burned with anger, knowing that these three men robbed my friend of the loving intimacy she deserved. I realized just how angry I was with men as well. Years of hearing stories of violence against women, and then this story in particular, made it hard for me to look at male groups the same way. I no longer wanted so desperately to be a part of them. I was tired of all the people with "boys will be boys" attitudes, who think that violence is something innate in males and hard-wired into their brains. I decided that my desperate search for masculinity was pointless and that it ultimately contributed to a stereotypical male culture that those three men used to justify their assault. I wanted to stand up at my next presentation and shout, "Men suck, and I want no part of their culture!"

Well, I didn't end up doing that, but I certainly thought about the previously mentioned song verse, "I thank God that I'm not a woman, but sometimes I wish I wasn't a man." I certainly agreed with the sentiment.

During the time when our students were trying to rally support for our program, something happened that shattered my cynicism. Robin wrote a letter to a campus administrator about the loss of the program and its significance to the university. She sent me a copy as well. Most of the other students' efforts focused on saving the direct crisis and intervention services of our victim advocates. Even I was more concerned about the loss of the victim advocate position than my educational component. This is why I wasn't quite prepared when I read Robin's letter.

With her journal entries depicting her hatred and distrust of men still fresh in my mind, I read Robin's words. "Heath has been one of my main inspirations. After my assault, I developed a hatred for men, but through Heath and all his wonderful work to raise awareness about violence against women and educate the campus and community, I was able to realize that all men are not bad."

I put down the letter and cried.

During all this time of being bitter and unjustly mad at men, I had failed to see the hope and healing of the woman right in front of me. I had started to dislike men, and I didn't want to be one. I spent most of my life trying to figure out what one was and had finally given up the effort altogether, but then I read her note. I finally learned what it was to be "a man," and I learned it from a rape survivor. Perhaps being "a man" (or "a woman" for that matter) has to do with our ability to stand side by side with people who are not like us, support them, and, most important, learn the lessons they have to offer. I know that higher education is supposed to be about the students, but I'm not an educator because of what I teach, I'm an educator because of what I learn.

As a result of this lesson, I recently picked up the masculinity I once threw away. It feels different now; it's less rigid than before. It's not perfect, but it is presentable. There is still a lot of work to do, and I sometimes still "wish I wasn't a man," but I have mellowed a bit, found the courage to forgive, and am proud of the man I've become, the men I work with, and the men who give a damn. I am most proud, however, of the women (like Robin) who inspire my work—women I never would have met had it not been for the wonderful years I spent at the Women's Center. I don't think I could live up to being a woman, so right now I'll work on being a man.

HOSPITALITY, CALVIN STYLE

BY

BOB CROW

On Wednesday, September 19, 2001, just eight days after the horrific events of 9/11, a voicemail message was left on an office phone at Calvin College in Grand Rapids, Mich. The voice on the message warned that in 36 hours, significant harm would occur on campus. It said something about lots of fire and devastation. The message was left at night, so it was not retrieved until the following morning.

College and local law enforcement officials worked to comprehend the disturbing message. Was this a legitimate threat? Could something really happen on our campus? In light of what had happened the previous week in New York and Washington, D.C., the college could not take this warning lightly. We interpreted the message to imply a bomb threat, and we decided that the campus needed to be completely evacuated by 10 p.m. that day, Thursday, September 20.

With care and precision, this organizational crisis was made nearly manageable. How could we accurately portray the seriousness of the situation, while not causing panic or undue fear? And with just four hours to empty the entire campus, what in the world would we do with the 2,400 residential students, approximately 50 percent of whom were from outside the state? It was a college official's nightmare.

At 6 p.m., teams of Student Life personnel went to each residence hall to present the information and inform students that they needed to evacuate the campus by 10 p.m. Expecting many not to know where to go or to have transportation, the college had asked employees if they would be willing to host students in their homes for the next day and a half. (I remember informing my wife of this, concluding that we could accommodate up to 15 students at our home.) As these teams explained the need for evacuation to students, we also informed them that there would be homes and transportation available for anyone who needed it. The plan was for these students to meet with "employee hosts" at our Campus Center promptly at 9 p.m. Anyone who needed a place would be cared for.

What happened next was nothing less than amazing. At 9 p.m., I went to the Campus Center. I found more than 100 employees gathered, ready to take adopted students home. Those employees, showing distinctive love for our students, waited until they had to leave campus at 10 p.m. All left without a student in tow.

That's right: Not one student needed to go home with a faculty or staff member or administrator. All the resident students took such care of one another that not one of them needed a place to stay. I remember hearing some say, "Anyone want to go to Canada for the weekend?" Another said, "No, we're going to Chicago. Anyone need a ride?" Off-campus students returned to campus to see if anyone needed a place to stay. One yelled out, "I live off-campus. We have six couches and plenty of room. If anyone needs a place to stay, come with me!" To be sure, since the closure of campus would include the entire day on Friday, it provided a nice impromptu holiday weekend.

But I still couldn't believe it. It was an amazing display of how our learning community could demonstrate care in the face of a very difficult set of circumstances. It was overwhelming to have witnessed all those employees ready to take students home with them. But even more amazing was that not one of those employees had anyone to take home. All had been cared for by fellow students in a remarkable display of hospitality, Calvin-style.

THE ENCOURAGEMENT FILE

BY

JENNIFER FONSECA

This past semester, a well-meaning student sent me a letter informing me that our "Project BEST" freshman seminar class was affectionately nicknamed "Project Worst." The student's editorial paragraphs continued with a barrage on the errors of the course. After receiving the letter, I skimmed a few paragraphs and set it aside...for about 3 weeks. I was not prepared to read the remaining comments.

Maybe if the student had printed the letter on pretty stationery or used colored ink, it would have eased the blow. Instead, there was sterile white paper with badgering black ink. I had knots in my neck and shoulders from skimming just a few paragraphs. The idea that "I am no good at what I do" raised its ugly head as I reflected on the words. I felt like a failure.

While sticks and stones don't break our bones, they sure leave bruises. After I read the letter, my bruised ego needed a lift. I remembered my special green hanging file. Everyone should have a green hanging file labeled "Encouragement" to save thank you notes written by students.

Sometimes encouragement comes in the form of a Post-It note saying, "You have blessed me more than I can say!" Other affirmations arrive following an answered question, such as, "I also wanted to thank you for all that you have done this semester. You, above all of my teachers, have truly showed that you care for us as people. Thanx for everything! Your fire is truly contagious." Every so often, a thoughtful card shows up on my desk. The rainbow-colored drawings on the envelope likely took more time than the actual handwritten note, yet together they convey the reminder of the positive difference I have made.

Nowadays, the more common form of encouragement is e-mail, which requires an interpreter. Although such e-mails might look like they consist of random strokes of keys clicked out by a toddler, they actually use the hieroglyphics of the Millennials. They might read something along the lines of :

> Professor, ?^, FWIW I wanted to tell U IMHO that U R OTH. TYVM for all U do. :) OBTW, TIA 4 the reference. (((((((Mrs. Fonseca)))))))))) Well, TAFN, CUL8R.

Which roughly translates as:

> What's up? For what it's worth, I wanted to tell you, in my humble opinion, that you are off the hook. Thank you very much for all you do. Smile. Oh, by the way, thanks in advance for the reference. Hug. Well, that's all for now, see you later.

After finding an interpreter for these e-mail notes, I think it is not so bad to get a note on white paper with black ink that simply reads, "I just wanted to let you know that I really admire you. Your willingness to serve by teaching us is greatly appreciated. Thank you so much." No interpreter needed.

On days when the sticks and stones are flying, it is a comfort to have the encouragement file nearby. Criticisms and complaints, regardless of how true they might be, can still hurt, so choose the antivirus of the encouragement file. Reading the notes of appreciation helped turn my thoughts around and remind me that despite the complaints, I really am OK.

ACADEMIC ADVISING SUCCESS STORIES

BY
THOMAS J. GRITES

The academic advising process in higher education is one that can blend the best of student affairs and academic affairs. Both faculty and student affairs professionals may provide this essential service. At times, this key opportunity is taken for granted and not recognized for its potential to motivate students to succeed. The following three stories from my experience exemplify the significance of a positive academic advising relationship. They demonstrate that academic advisors with the right blend of information sharing and genuine concern for students can make all the difference in their academic success.

> *Raymond*
> Hello, sir. Just for your information, I just completed Ethics in America, and I am sure I earned an A or a B+. That will fulfill my final graduation requirement…Once again, thank you very much for all of your time and help. It has been a pleasure having you as an advisor (e-mail correspondence received December 9, 2004).

I was not Raymond's official advisor. Actually, I never met Raymond. I was an advisor charged with facilitating his graduation. Several years back, Raymond was suspended from the campus because of a felony conviction. He served his sentence and desperately wanted to complete his degree. Raymond needed only two more courses, but he was not permitted to enter the campus grounds without informing the campus police and receiving an escort.

In my administrative capacity, I knew of a policy that enabled students this close to graduation to complete their requirements under their original degree plan. This policy was exercised, and we scheduled his two distance education courses. I complied with all campus and academic policies, and Raymond met the curricular requirements. I would do the same for any student trying to complete a degree in a difficult situation. This story is important because it exemplifies the need to help all students. Some might question our institution's support of Raymond, but I saw the attainment of his bachelor's degree as significant for his future. Raymond trusted me and was confident that I wanted him to succeed. Though I never had face-to-face contact with Raymond, I gained his trust, respected it, and did what I could to help him earn his degree.

Randall

It took a little more time to graduate but it's finally over. I want to thank you for all of your support, confidence, and help in this achievement. It's now just sinking in after receiving word on my achievement and completion of the courses needed to graduate. If I could do it again I would definitely do it the same way, playing soccer and achieving all the goals, situations and pressure being a student athlete that is really overlooked. But the only thing I would change is having you as my preceptor earlier to stay and push me to graduate on time. Thanks for everything and I can't wait to shake your hand on the 30th (e-mail correspondence received January 16, 2004).

Randall was a high-risk student academically. In fact, he never expected to attend college, but his mother and our soccer coach persuaded him to try it. He struggled in the classroom but persisted. Although I knew of him because I am a soccer fan, I never really met him until his senior year of athletic eligibility. This was the year his soccer team won the men's Division III national championship. His soccer career was over, but he was still a year away from graduation.

After the season was over and all the accolades were received, Randall was left to complete his degree. I was not Randall's official advisor either, but we got to know each other through soccer. I encouraged him to come see me to determine exactly what he needed in order to graduate. He did so, and we worked together for the next year to complete his degree.

This story is also significant to me because Randall knew I cared. I built a relationship with him, respected the demands on him both inside and outside the classroom, and believed in his ability to complete his degree. Knowing that Randall was quite introverted, I often sought him out to make sure he was doing what was necessary to complete his degree. I know my relationship with Randall significantly contributed to his graduation—a perceived improbable goal when he enrolled.

Matthew

You may not remember me but my name is Matthew and I was very fortunate enough to take one of your education classes. This letter is long overdue but I wanted to take this opportunity to say thank you.

Two months before I started my student teaching, I ran into you in the hallway. You stopped and we had a brief conversation. You asked me where I planned to do my student teaching. I mentioned that I was looking at a 7th-and-8th-grade school. You paused and asked what level of students I would like to eventually teach. I stated high school students, and you informed me that maybe I should change my school choices to include high schools and not junior highs. You told me that student teaching in a high school setting might increase my chances of getting a high school job, not to mention it would give me a 'taste' of high school life. We shook hands and you went on your way.

I changed my school choices to include a high school (based on your recommendation). As luck would have it, I got that school, and halfway through my student teaching experience, I landed a full-time job as the new English/journalism teacher where I have been teaching for the past three years. Furthermore, I went on to be the advisor for the Mock Trial Team and Debate Team and the Webmaster of that school. Finally, I am also the secretary of the professional development committee.

Because you took the time to talk with me and because you cared, I am where I am today. Thank you so much for your guidance and wisdom. I could never forget that advice you gave me that day. I think about where I would be if you had just simply passed me by with nothing more than a hand wave, and it scares me. I am everything I always wanted to be, and you helped make that possible. Thank you from the bottom of my heart. You made a difference in my life and I am forever grateful. I hope you continue to instruct and guide students, and I wish you the best of luck (e-mail correspondence received March 8, 2003).

I gave Matthew simple academic advice that I'm sure any knowledgeable person would have given. I cherish Matthew's story because it reminds me of the potential in any impromptu, informal conversation with a student. Because I took the time to talk and inquire about Matthew's well-being, he heeded my advice and, as a result, landed his ideal position. Matthew's story also reminds me that there are times when I will never really know if, how, or when my time, suggestions, and advice will have an impact on a student. In his case, I found out 3 years later.

These stories are only a few from my experiences as an academic advisor. Many more surely exist involving advisors on every campus. The important message is to recognize the potential of academic advising, regardless of its reporting line, the personnel used to provide it, and the location or context in which it occurs. These stories demonstrate the complex roles of those engaged in academic advising—informational, relational, and conceptual. Knowledge of institutional policies and the relationship between the curriculum and workplace are evident in the stories of Raymond and Matthew, respectively. Above all, the relational aspects of building trust and confidence are evident in all three stories. I am proud to know that I helped these students and others like them. I also never underestimate the potential of each student interaction.

LISTENING TO YOUR INNER VOICE
BY
SARAH M. MARSHALL

I share with you my personal journal of self-discovery to highlight the importance of discovering one's calling. While my student affairs career eventually led me to the professoriate, I include this essay to encourage others to reflect on their purpose in life. I hope my example reinforces your acknowledged calling or challenges you to critically examine that which gives your life meaning.

I, like many, entered student affairs as an active student leader. I loved the collegiate setting and the opportunity to interact daily with students. While I enjoyed my eight years as a student affairs practitioner, I knew that I needed something different.

They say that hindsight is 20/20. I had my first teaching experience as a senior in college. I co-facilitated a section of emerging leaders and loved it. As a result, in each subsequent professional position, I sought the opportunity to teach in some way, but I didn't really view it as teaching—it was more like facilitating workshops. Need someone to teach University 101? No problem. Can I start a leadership series here even though I'm already overextended? No problem. I even remember calling the local community college to see if I could volunteer to teach its University 101 course and being greatly disappointed to learn that I had to be an employee of the college to do so.

I share this story with you because as a faculty member who truly believes she has found her calling, I know from experience the importance of listening to your inner voice. Listen to yourself and recognize what you truly enjoy, what gives your life meaning. Once your motives are sincere, you can give yourself permission to pursue your dreams.

As a dutiful wife, I left my position as a director of student activities and followed my husband when his career took him from Chicago to Oklahoma. The trade-off was that I wouldn't work. I'd finish my dissertation and have a baby. Three months after my arrival, I finished my comprehensive exams, was pregnant, and had a new position as the director of student activities and student union at the local university. So much for making plans!

Again, something wasn't quite right. The position was satisfying, but at times I would drag myself out of bed. I gave birth to my first daughter 6 months after arriving at the university. While I wasn't excited to return to work three months later, I did so for two reasons: to prove that women do come back to work after maternity leave (it was an ongoing debate among the leadership as to whether the university should have hired a pregnant woman) and, while I loved my daughter, I missed the collegiate environment and the students.

Three months after my return from maternity leave, a faculty colleague at a neighboring research university approached me about a one-year visiting assistant professor position in its higher education program. I was shocked. I couldn't be a faculty member. I was a student affairs professional. I couldn't go over to "the other side." Who was I to teach other professionals? What did I have to offer? I wasn't qualified to teach anyone.

I remember e-mailing my academic mentor for her advice. I did so thinking she was going to laugh at me or tell me that I wasn't qualified. On the contrary, she encouraged me to apply and even sent a copy of her vita (since I had no idea what one was) and a list of interview questions for me to consider. I was stunned. To this day, I don't know if she realized how vulnerable I was at that point in my life. I was professionally unsatisfied but didn't believe in myself or my ability to do anything else. Rather than question my motives or my abilities, she praised me and helped me recognize my potential. I mention her role because I think it's important not only that we look deep within ourselves to recognize our calling but also that we realize the impact we can have helping others discover theirs.

To my amazement, I was offered the faculty appointment. I accepted and prepped most of the summer. I walked in the first day to 25 higher education graduate students, most of whom were older and probably wiser than me. Overly prepared, I showed up with shaking hands and a bribe of brownies and facilitated my first graduate-level course. I was hooked. I loved the challenge of the classroom. I loved learning with the students. I loved encouraging them to think about things in different ways. I loved the debate, the banter, the engagement. I loved it when they told me that their heads hurt from thinking too much.

I also appreciated the advising. Of course, with my student affairs background, I was eager to advise and even mentor students. I felt appreciated for the time I took to talk with students—to discuss dissertation topics, complete their academic plans, or offer suggestions for managing career, school, and family.

Another major component of my professional life is my commitment to research. Initially, I had the same anxieties. My original line of research focused on the ways that higher education administrators manage work and family. It wasn't until I presented the findings from my dissertation research that I understood why we do research. It was my first national presentation. The room was full of women eager to hear about how others had managed both a successful career in student affairs and a family. The questions wouldn't stop coming. Our session ran over and even spilled out into the hallway. Women thanked me, gave me their business cards, and asked for copies of my work. One mother, with an infant in tow, approached me in tears to thank me. That's what it's all about. I don't want to write things that are in obscure journals that no one reads. I want to help others, and my research is one way to do that.

That's what motivates me.

I think it is important to know where I've been to understand the next part of my calling. While I remain true to my vocation, there are times when a calling can be challenged. Although I know deep down that teaching new professionals is my passion and my way to meaningfully contribute to student affairs and higher education, at times I wonder about my longevity in the field.

With the birth of my second daughter, my husband and I decided to move closer to family. Since faculty appointments in higher education and students affairs are typically harder to come by than medical sales positions, we decided that I would secure employment first. Eventually, I accepted a new faculty appointment in Michigan. I was recruited to help grow our university's higher education program and add an emphasis in student affairs. I knew that it would be a challenge to grow a program in a state that already had many strong higher education programs, but I was told that we had the support of the president, dean, and department.

I quickly realized the first challenge would not be to enhance the program but to dig it out of a hole. Our enrollments were low, and our departmental reputation on campus was less than stellar. While my colleagues tried to be supportive, most had K-12 backgrounds and believed that the higher education and student affairs students should take the same classes as the students who planned to be principals and superintendents because it's all education. I often explained to them that they were trying to fit a square peg into a round hole, but my untenured pleas fell on deaf, tenured ears.

I also quickly discovered that the students were not used to rigor in their classes. Students complained that I required more than one book, that they actually had to read for my classes, and that an independent research project at the end of the semester was more than anyone had previously asked of them.

Reality hit when I walked into my first class. Again I was overly prepared and my hands were a little shaky, but I left the brownies at home. To my surprise, I only had five students when I was used to at least 15. Two were international students. Of the five, only one was in higher education—the other four just needed a class to graduate. Talk about a challenging semester! I also found that returning to my home state meant a loss of anonymity. In my other class, I discovered that one of the students and I attended my undergraduate alma mater at the same time. Let's just say that it was a bit awkward when he disclosed some of my college antics to the rest of the class. I like to think that his revelation made me more of a real person to them.

Midway through the semester, I started to wonder if this was truly my purpose in life. Maybe I should have stayed at home with my children. Maybe I should go back into administration. I really didn't need the headaches, constant worry, and daily battles. In late October, during one of my lowest points, I went to my campus mailbox and found a note from Maria, one of my former students. I don't share this to say, "Wow, look at me, I'm great," but to reinforce the fact that we all have Marias in our lives. They help remind us of our commitment and give us hope. She wrote:

> Dr. Marshall–
>
> I hope this card finds you safe and happy. I know I said it before, but you really did change my life. I am so blessed to have met you and to have learned from you. You will always be my motivating light, and words can never express my gratitude. Thank you for being my teacher, my mentor and my friend. Your kindness will never be forgotten. I wish you all the best in life!
>
> Sincerely,
> Maria

That's when I realized, whether I have 25 students or five, I can make a difference. I know that I need to stay true to my calling. I constantly remind myself to be patient, maintain my standards for student performance, conduct and present the research that I love, and to remember that my life has meaning.

In student affairs we are challenged daily. There are ups and downs, times we love our work and times we hate it, times we appreciate students and times we want to strangle them. I hope my story inspires you to reflect on your calling, your purpose in life. I encourage you to truly listen to your inner voice.

Consider what is important to you, what gives your life meaning, and follow your heart. It won't be perfect—nothing ever is—but it is often the challenging times that make us stronger, better, and more dedicated. Regularly remind yourself why you do what you do. Recall the Marias in your life. Remember the significance of your work. Stay true to yourself and to your calling.

WHAT I LEARNED FROM A CHILD

BY

ROBERT GLENN

I had an opportunity in the summer of 2005 to reflect upon my career as I was attending the NASPA Region III Summer Symposium in San Antonio, Texas. San Antonio was where I spent the formative years of my youth. One afternoon, I was alone on the River Walk and began to consider the circumstances that brought me to this point. While I would like to believe that I entered the profession of student affairs with forethought and careful consideration, I have to admit that, like many of my colleagues, I backed into the field through chance and happenstance. I believe advancing to my current position, however, was the result of a number of deliberate steps. Nonetheless, chance played a real part in helping me find a profession that is one of the centerpieces of my life. One of these chance events had particular impact on me.

I can't remember what I was doing awake at 2 in the morning, but I was a hall director in a men's hall. Do I need to explain any further? The TV was on. I was watching *The Untouchables*. During a commercial break, a message about the Big Brothers/Big Sisters volunteer program came on. At that moment, it occurred to me that I could volunteer. Over the next couple of days, the more I thought about being a Big Brother, the more convinced I was that I should volunteer.

Honestly, I convinced myself to do the right thing but for all the wrong reasons. I thought about what being a Big Brother could do for me. I was working on a graduate degree in counseling, and I reasoned that being a Big Brother would be good practice. I was an R.A. and now a hall director, so I had all the good "people training" that would make the one-on-one stuff easy to manage. I was single, and I thought about how women love sensitive guys. I envisioned myself in various situations where a woman would come up to me when I was with my Little Brother. "What an adorable little boy," they would coo. "I'm a Big Brother and this is my Little Brother," I would respond in my "Aw, shucks, it ain't nuthin'" kind of Will Rogers way. And then the women would look at me and think, "What a great guy!"

I would like to believe that somewhere deep down inside, I was motivated to help a child in the same way that so many others helped me growing up. I had been mentored, and now it was time to be a mentor. I had certainly received more than my fair share of help. There were folks like my first R.A., affectionately referred to as "Aunt Charlie." There was the women's hall director with whom I had long and meaningful discussions about life and philosophy. There were the dean and associate dean of students who chose me to be an R.A., put me through hours of training, and later hired me to be a hall director and then coordinator. The truth was that I didn't consciously think of any of these role models. I was self-absorbed and thought only of the personal benefits.

The Big Brothers/Big Sisters selection and matching process, while long and somewhat complicated, was no real problem. The matching process finally came down to a choice among three types of boys. Big Brothers/Big Sisters could match me with a boy who was relatively problem-free. Then they had boys who had some problems but weren't too much of a risk. Finally, they had the more challenging boys. Being matched with one of these boys would require real commitment and patience. Once again my self-absorbed arrogance overwhelmed any natural intelligence I possessed. Arrogantly, I thought, "Hey, I'm working on a master's degree in counseling. I'm not the average guy. I can handle the tough cases. They probably have a hard time matching these kids. I'll give one of them a break and be his Big Brother." So I told the counselor to give me his toughest case.

Fortunately for me, my counselor just smiled and said, "Let me tell you about Jim." Jim was 9 and had patiently waited for a Big Brother for two years. Jim was a slow learner, and others were reluctant to be matched with him. He lived with his mother, grandmother, and younger sister. A time was set for us to meet.

A first meeting between a Big Brother and a Little Brother is usually a well-choreographed affair. I was scheduled to meet with Jim's mother, who would have veto power if she didn't approve of me. After this meeting, a time was arranged for me to meet Jim. Little did I know that our encounter would forever change me and the way that I look at the world.

Our meeting seemed unremarkable. Jim said very little, was intensely shy, and just looked at me. It was suggested that for our first meeting, we get ice cream and talk about what we would do on our first "official" outing. We got into the car and drove off into the dark, rainy night. We were about halfway to the store, and I was making small talk. Quite suddenly, Jim began to cry. I was caught completely off-guard. My arrogance, which had given me so much courage, gave way to panic. I was alone with a crying child. My residence life training had prepared me for many different kinds of crises, but I was totally unprepared for this. I reached over, put my hand on his knee, and tried to comfort him. "Jim," I said, "Are you all right?"

As suddenly as Jim began to cry, he grabbed my hand just as tightly as he could. He looked up at me with his tearful eyes. He said, "Big brudder, I love you."

Even now, more than 20 years later, I cannot think of this event without being moved. I did nothing to deserve this pledge of affection. I hadn't even bought him an ice cream cone. I didn't deserve his devotion and couldn't fathom how just showing up was worthy of anything.

We began our weekly tradition. I would arrive at Jim's house and he would jump into my car, almost before I could stop. We would go for walks, play games, play catch, or even just watch TV together. At the end of our time, I would take Jim home and we would have the same conversation.

"What do you want to do next week, Jim?"

"I dunno, Big Brudder, what do you want to do?" "I don't know, Jim. Why don't we just wait and see what we feel like. Is that OK with you?"

"That's OK, Big Brudder."

The next weekend would arrive, and we would always think of something to do.

After a few months, I thought it was time for me start taking some "therapeutic" actions. Surely there were specially designed games or activities I should be engaging in with Jim to "improve" him. I called his psychologist to find out what kind of special activities I should plan. The psychologist sounded a little surprised. "You're kidding, aren't you? Just relax. The difference in his condition now compared to before you two were together is like the difference between night and day. Just keep doing exactly what you are doing. Don't change a thing."

It would be a long time before I learned the simple lesson Jim was teaching. Although I was pretty thick-headed, Jim was very patient with me. Slowly, during the four years we were together, he brought me to a new level of understanding. I began to understand that you never accomplish anything of real merit or worth when your only thoughts are of yourself. When you take yourself out of the picture, it is possible to see others and what they really need. I couldn't see what Jim needed because I couldn't look past myself. Once I did, I learned other simple lessons that aid me today.

I believe that Alexander Astin said it best in *Achieving Educational Excellence.* In essence, he said that the traditional measures we use to judge the merit of a university are just measures of reputation, not excellence. It doesn't matter how many degrees your faculty members have or how state-of-the-art your buildings are or how many volumes are in the library. What really denotes a quality institution is whether it can take students from where they are to where they want to be. In other words, when a university can look beyond itself, it can see its students. When we can really see our students, we can measure their needs. When we take care of their needs, we help them get to where they want to be. I believe that when we boil down other works, like *The Student Personnel Point of View* or *Learning Reconsidered*, we get to the same basic lesson: We need to look beyond ourselves and see our students. When we take care of their needs, our needs as professionals will be met.

As I sat there on the River Walk in my old hometown, it occurred to me that I was pretty lucky that Jim came along early in my career and set me on the right path. I hope that I have returned the favor by passing that lesson along to others. We'll see.

References

American Council on Education. (1937 & 1949). *The student personnel point of view: A report of the conference on the philosophy and development of student personnel work in colleges and universities.* http://www.myacpa.org/pub/pub_ar.cfm

National Association of Student Personnel Administrators, & American College Personnel Association. (2004, January). *Learning reconsidered: A campus-wide focus on the student experience.*
http://www.myacpa.org/pub/documents/LearningReconsidered.doc

LESSONS LEARNED

CHARIOT RACES

BY

JIM D. HARDWICK

As the new fraternity and sorority advisor on a mostly Greek campus, I found myself expressing concerns to the Greek Week planning committee about the chariot races that were traditionally held during Greek Week. The chariots, constructed the week of the race, consisted of a flat cart with a push bar in the back. Two fraternity men and one sorority woman would run at full speed pushing the cart, on which sat another sorority woman, down a city street to the finish line. The chariot had no brakes, no steering wheel, no seat belt, and no safety inspections.

I thought the presentation of my concerns regarding the safety of the chariot races would result in a unanimous decision by the committee to cancel the event. Unfortunately, I was wrong.

Instead, I was besieged by requests to not cancel the event. The feedback came from members of the planning committee, chapter officers, the Interfraternity Council, and the Panhellenic Council. All lobbied me to allow the chariot races for one last Greek Week. The students acknowledged my concerns about safety but begged for one more chance to run the race. Against my better judgment, I agreed. At the time, I reasoned that the chariot races had run for years without any serious incident. I also questioned whether I was trying to change too much too fast on the campus as the new fraternity and sorority advisor. I took the sage advice that I had received in graduate school: Sometimes you have to pick your battles.

Greek Week arrived, and the campus was full of excitement. I was standing at the midpoint of the chariot races course when I saw the accident happen. The sorority woman on one of the chariots flipped off the chariot in a huge arc and landed headfirst on the pavement. Her neck twisted abruptly on contact, and she crumpled unconscious onto the street. An ambulance was called, and the woman was removed from the street on a backboard. I followed the ambulance to the hospital in my vehicle, alternately praying for her and taking myself to task for allowing the fraternity and sorority leaders to talk me out of canceling the races.

When I arrived at the hospital, I grabbed the local phonebook to notify the sorority chapter's advisor and my supervisor at the college of the accident. I prayed nonstop for the woman. I knew that the fact that the event would not be

134

repeated in future years would offer no comfort to this woman or her parents. I made a lot of promises to myself and to God in the emergency room waiting room. Foremost was that if the student and I both survived this incident and I remained in student affairs, I would not let students talk me into holding an event when I had concerns about safety.

The woman regained consciousness, and the medical staff at the hospital found no injuries. Apparently, her inebriation level had made her movements so fluid that, as she hit the pavement, the trauma to the neck and spine had been minimized. She had a few scrapes but would be released to her parents after a few hours of observation at the hospital.

The lessons I took from the chariot races have helped me several times during my career in student affairs. I have talked students out of sponsoring boxing matches, mud wrestling, all-night raves, a Houdini-like escape while submerged in a lake, and re-opening an abandoned ski hill. The time and the place to review a decision ripe with risk management issues are around a table with colleagues you trust during the workday, not late at night at a sorority house with an enthusiastic group of students. I also learned that the discussion with the students needs to go beyond issues of personal safety because, too often, students are willing to risk their own safety. The discussion needs to address participant safeguards, event safeguards, chapter liability, and institutional liability. As a student affairs administrator, I need to reserve the right of the institution to make a decision to protect the institution. Through the years, I have learned to trust my intuition as a risk manager when I find myself in situations with students who are excitedly telling me about their idea for an event that reminds me of chariot races.

YOU CAN'T WIN THEM ALL...
BUT GO ON ANYWAY

BY
SHANNON ELLIS

I never much cared for students. After all, they're whiney complainers who never like the food, think studying the basic humanities is a waste of time, and believe higher education should be free—books too!

"Just tell me what to take...," is all we seem to hear in academic advising, and when we don't tell them exactly what classes to take and when, we are accused of bad advising. All they want to do is check off boxes on the requirement page—or rather, they want me to check off the boxes for them. After all, if I have heard it once, I have heard it a thousand times: "I just wanna get outta here..." I am unsure if any learning is going on, with their resistance to learning the facts and forming their own mindset. Those are the mainstream students. Be honest. If you've worked for more than a day in this field, you know I am right.

OK, they aren't all bad, but it would have been easy to think so the year Connolly Hastings (pseudonym) became our student body president. The position is very prestigious and influential, not just on campus but around the state. Regents, chancellors, legislators, and the governor listen to our student body leaders.

Connolly was a nightmare student. She proudly described herself as smart, lazy, unwilling to learn the facts, lacking what I call a moral compass, most nervous when she had to speak in public, and driven by money.

With all these qualifications, she sought a job from me. Never mind that I didn't have any campus jobs available—she wanted me to just make one up at a handsome starting salary and hire her: "Shannon, make it happen."

And let's not even go into the times she was outraged by her parking tickets. Eventually, they totaled more than $100, which made it impossible for her to register for classes. I'll admit I was tempted to pay them off just to help her graduate and leave my life. When she finished berating the university for having such stupid rules, she asked me what to do. I said, "Pay your tickets." Click. The phone went dead at the other end.

I always ask our new student leaders what they want to leave as a legacy of their time in this role. I ask them to be innovative, to dream and stretch. I offer all my support and that of others to help them leave this mark on the campus. I've helped them build a new student union, bring world leaders to our little campus, successfully lobby the legislature for millions of dollars in student aid, and dramatically diversify a 130-year-old Western traditions curriculum. What was Connolly's answer to my legacy question? "Get alcohol back in the fraternities."

No vision is one thing. Lying and leading others to do likewise is quite another. Confront I did, sometimes with attorneys in tow, always in private and never in public. Connolly's first act, after everyone left for the summer, was to undo everything prior leaders had done. So I thought, "Things will get better when the others return in the fall." I was wrong. They wanted this woman to lead them in these new ways of mistrust and autonomy. There was even momentum behind her plan to fire all the staff funded by the student government, never mind state personnel rules and processes.

This is not a story of how she "came around." I am not about to tell you the tale of how she eventually learned from my endless lessons and tough-love stances. She reacted to them with screaming and yelling, stomping out of the room, hanging up the phone, writing nasty letters to the newspaper, and phoning my boss and my boss's boss. She always went straight to the top, saying, "I don't deal with minions." When she got to the top, I watched her look into the eyes of the president or chancellor and say, "You don't have any right to tell me what to do."

This story is about what I learned from her.

First, do not cower or bend to hostile student leaders' tactics and demeanor. Neither you nor your staff should tolerate being berated or belittled by the student leadership.

Second, treat them as you would any other elected student leader. Do not coddle or favor. Do teach and advise even when it is unwanted—especially when it is unwanted.

Third, be true to yourself. Be true to the style you have developed with students. Remain committed to their growth and development and pursue them in the ways you have always wanted to help them learn.

Fourth, realize that while you cannot change them, you can change yourself. When I came to this realization is when I started to think and write about what I was learning from her. What if she were right about everything? How could I hang onto my clear professional values and love of the profession while continuing to work with this leader who was so different from anything I had ever encountered?

Fifth, do not succumb to the temptation to ignore them. When they hang up on you, call back. When they stomp off in a huff, go after them.

Sixth, love them. In coming to this decision, I was overcome by a mild sense of peace that channeled my energies into what I could do with Connolly and not how to work against her all the time.

Seventh, confront them. I never let her off the hook. I went home at night able to face myself in the mirror, knowing I had done my job working with this student and developing leader.

Eighth, never meet with them alone. Always keep a journal of meetings and phone calls, even when you just left a message. Connolly's favorite tactic was to say, "You never called me back." When she said that once, a quick flip of my "Connolly blue notebook" revealed that I had returned the 2:20 p.m. call on December 17, 2004, at 4:12 p.m. that day and left a message on her cell.

Ninth, never give up. I knew I could not make it work, but I tried to until she walked across the stage at commencement.

Tenth, never expect them to come back in a year or five or ten and tell you that you were right and they were wrong. It is not going to happen. You did your best. You can't win them all, and plenty of students are waiting to lead. They need your love, advice, and honest guidance.

UNEXPECTED HEART ATTACK

BY

JIM D. HARDWICK

I awoke from a deep sleep when I heard someone pounding on the front door of our house. I jumped out of bed and looked at the clock on the bedside table. It read 3 a.m. I was incredulous that anyone would be pounding on our door at this hour of night except for some dire emergency. I pulled on the T-shirt and sweatpants that I usually left beside my bed as a habit from years of working in a residence hall. I ran to the front door of our house, not knowing what to expect.

At the front door, I turned on the outside light. I looked through the window of the door and was stunned to see a group of people gathered on our front lawn. I opened the door to hear the group yell at the top of their voices, "You've just had a heart attack!"

As the group ran to their cars parked along our street, I saw that our front lawn had been decorated with paper hearts on stakes. The paper hearts had positive messages on them, I discovered later. The "heart attack" that the group had yelled about loudly enough to wake up our neighbors referred not to the pounding in my chest but to the brightly colored heart-shaped decorations.

By this point, it had dawned on me that the fleeing individuals leaving our front yard were members of our student housing staff, whom my wife and I had hosted for dinner at our house earlier in the evening.

I stood in the doorway, unsure how to react. I noticed my wife and my 7-year-old daughter standing behind me. The "heart attack" awoke them from their sleep, too. I knew our alarm clock was set to ring in 3 hours. I was acutely aware of how the noise might have disrupted our neighbors. I wondered if our neighbors were lying awake in bed, looking at their alarm clocks and regretting having a college administrator move into the neighborhood.

The next day, the hall directors from student housing appeared in my office door, curious to find out how I had liked my "heart attack." I knew this was one of those teachable moments that I wanted to handle well so as not to dampen their spirits or the opening of the school year. I cited all of the positives I could muster. I told them that I appreciated the team effort, and that the "heart attack" was a very creative stunt. I understood that it must have been difficult to keep the student staff awake that late during housing staff training week. I understood that their gesture was meant as a thank you for the dinner we hosted. I told them we had enjoyed having them and their staffs to our house for dinner. I said that I appreciated the positive messages that were written on the hearts.

For next time, I gently suggested, I would appreciate a group activity or thank you that would not wake up my neighbors. From the looks on their faces, I realized that they had not even considered that possibility. From their earlier comments, I could tell that the students were excited about pulling off the stunt. I cautioned them to consider that what they as professional staff role-models viewed as appropriate activities or boundaries could come back to them in unexpected stunts pulled on them by their student staff or residents. Again, I could tell by their faces that the possibility of future stunts pulled on them was not a reality they had considered. I thanked the hall directors for coming over to our house for dinner and asked them to thank the student housing staff for the positive messages on the hearts. I wanted to be sure that the message taken back about the unexpected heart attack was that the positive messages on the hearts had been appreciated and unanticipated. For their messages, not their timing, I was very grateful.

GROWING THROUGH EXPERIENCES
WITH ADVERSITY

BY
BOB MOSIER

Many times in student affairs, the greatest growth occurs through overcoming adversity. Striving to deal with difficult situations while maintaining a positive outlook, can be a continuing struggle for those in the field. We deal with many challenges on a daily basis, some of which don't turn out quite as well as we had hoped. However, we persevere, overcoming obstacles in our quest to be more complete persons and successful in our work with others. I have learned many lessons from my own personal and professional experiences in dealing with adversity. As I have struggled to make meaning from the events, I have found that the human spirit will prevail with an always hopeful optimism about the future.

One of the biggest challenges I faced in overcoming professional adversity occurred as part of fall training during a professional retreat in northern Wisconsin. Each fall, prior to the beginning of the academic year, the residential living staff would engage in team building, set goals, and discuss plans for the future at the retreat. As the retreat coordinator, one of my responsibilities was to pull a rack of canoes, via a trailer, from our campus location in central Wisconsin. The canoes were an important part of the retreat, as participants looked forward to paddling out on one of the lakes during recreation time to take in the beautiful setting.

A recently-hired residential living staff member accompanied me on this trip. She was an outstanding professional, having served in leadership positions in the Upper Midwest Region–Association of College and University Housing Officers (UMR–ACUHO), as well as having professional experience at several universities. It was my hope that we could develop rapport while riding together in the trailer.

My First Professional Challenge Of the Trip
My first professional challenge of the trip presented itself when I attempted, by myself, to back the trailer down a long, narrow incline behind the University Center, where I was to load the canoes. For those who do not know, backing up a trailer is a counter-intuitive process. You need to turn in the opposite direction from what seems logical in order to straighten out the trailer. While I am very

intuitive, I am definitely challenged at counter-intuitive activities. During the first half hour of trying to back the trailer down the incline, I began to realize some of my limitations in this area. After the second half hour, I began to think that perhaps the most efficient method of getting the trailer down the incline would be to just release it and let it find its own way to the bottom. I was quite certain that the wall at the end of the incline would stop it at approximately the right place. However, reason prevailed, and I was able to eventually maneuver the trailer, get the canoes loaded, and meet the new staff member for the trip north.

My Second Professional Challenge Of the Trip
The trip proved uneventful until we arrived at the retreat center, where I seemed to suffer from a heightened lack of reasonable decision-making. This would result in my second professional challenge. As we pulled into the center, I noticed that the location for dropping off the canoes involved a fairly tight turn around a shelter for parked vehicles. As I began to slowly and carefully turn around the shelter, I suddenly discovered that my forward progress was being impeded. It felt like something had caught onto part of the vehicle or the canoe rack.

The new staff member suggested that I get out of the van and check to see what was caught. I, however, chose a slightly different option, employing what I, at that moment, felt to be the most efficient method of getting unstuck: I gunned the motor and roared ahead. This was certainly leadership in action, overcoming challenges, forging new paths of discovery, and quickly moving toward the goal of getting the canoes unloaded. Much to our dismay, it turned out that the canoe rack was hooked onto the roof of the shelter! When I gunned the motor, I got the rack unstuck, but suffered several setbacks. I damaged part of the shelter roof, pulled down a fire lane sign, and bent the canoe rack into an interesting, and I thought, quite artistic new design. The new staff member seemed mildly stunned by this turn of events. She quickly recovered and had several new suggestions for me, including areas for personal and professional growth. The manager of the retreat center also weighed in with suggestions on how I might improve my future performance.

My Third Professional Challenge On The Trip
While the rest of the retreat went quite well, there was a slight concern in the back of my mind about getting the canoes back on the rack (still bent into an interesting angle), and returning them unharmed to our campus. I would also need to explain to several people back on campus how I had managed to damage the rack. While the new staff member seemed to have lost some of her initial confidence in my abilities, we did make it back to campus with the canoes intact. The happy ending to this story is that when I explained my plight with the canoe rack, one staff member of building services within residential living said

that he could fix the rack as good as new. With only minor surgery and major welding, he did just that.

Overcoming Personal Adversity
During this same time period, I experienced several personal challenges that involved adverse situations in and around mine and my wife's home. First, I inadvertently ran over with my lawn mower a small metal stake that marked the boundary of our yard. That action resulted in a bent crankshaft. Although the impact was not high-speed, it sounded like an airplane had crashed in our yard. This action certainly got the attention of my wife and our neighbors.

Second, while clearing the driveway of snow (a Wisconsin tradition), I tried cleaning the snow blower chute with the motor running, which seemed more efficient than turning the motor off. Using a snow shovel handle, I jammed the handle down into the chute. The vibration traveled up the handle, split the plastic blade in half, and shot that half of the blade 20 feet into the air. I once again found myself having to explain very unusual events to an increasingly skeptical wife.

Finally, in an attempt to use our washing machine more efficiently, I loaded 18 towels all at once. I thought this was a very creative way to save water and, thereby, increase the sustainability of our natural resources. This, however, did not work out quite as I had intended. After a short time, the towels absorbed all of the water in the washer. This caused the washer behave erratically. It started to vibrate strongly, leaving its agreed upon spot against the wall to march down the hallway. Fortunately, my wife was able to corral the washer and unplug it before it did any structural damage to our home. The washer eventually recovered from this trauma.

Lessons Learned from Overcoming Adversity
1. Slow down the decision-making process. Overemphasizing efficiency may or may not lead to greater effectiveness. While this may seem counterintuitive, I have been working to practice more counter-intuition, as well as the plain, garden variety intuition. A number of my adversity experiences seem to flow from my intent to be efficient without considering fully all of the ramifications of my actions. Many times, slowing down my decision-making process has led to greater success in achieving my goals.

2. Practice environmental scanning before, during, and after implementation of plans. It never hurts to stop and scan the environment. Sometimes, things that are not always readily visible, like a metal boundary marker, will jump out of the weeds to interfere with your objectives. Scanning the environment on a periodic basis can be very helpful in spotting obstacles before you run into them.

3. Engage in "stop action" exercises. Even when things are going well, it is helpful to build in time to assess how things are going and to identify problems before they grow too large to manage. For instance, an excellent time for a "stop action" exercise was when the canoe rack became stuck on the roof of the shelter. Whether stuck on a roof or stuck on some other problem, it is helpful to stop and assess how things are going, before proceeding too quickly into the direct action phase of the project.

4. Actively seek out the talents and expertise of others. Many times, the expertise of others that I have worked with has been invaluable in solving difficult problems. There are many individuals in the student affairs field with highly specialized expertise (such as welding canoe racks), that when called upon, can offer precious assistance. We all have times where we need advice or instruction on how to best operate complicated machinery, like the snow blower or the washing machine. Seeking out advice prior to operation can save you time and heartache in the end.

5. Listen carefully to others and absorb their feedback. I have learned a great deal throughout my professional career by listening to others and absorbing their life lessons. Some of these lessons have come from mentors, some from family, some from other professionals, and some from students. There is a great wealth of ideas and knowledge to be acquired by just stopping and listening to others. My only regret is that I did not always follow this piece of advice as well or as thoroughly as I could have in certain circumstances.

6. Ask yourself often, "What is my goal and how can I most effectively accomplish it?" If your goal involves working with other people to produce positive outcomes, it is very helpful to involve them in the planning and the process of achieving the goal. People are strongly motivated to do their best when they participate in the planning and decision-making process.

7. Visualize obstacles and brainstorm alternatives to overcome them. Many situations can be dealt with more effectively by spending time visualizing the challenge to be overcome and addressing it from a number of different angles. This way, one can preview the possible outcomes if various alternatives are chosen. For instance, it would have been helpful if I had visualized what might have occurred had I kept the snow blower motor running when clearing the clogged chute, and what might have occurred had I turned it off.

8. Rebound from adversity. Life is full of adversity. Many situations that don't have an immediate positive outcome can have a positive impact on a person's thinking and decision-making. Some of my best learning has come from making mistakes and then processing what I could do differently in the future to better deal with a challenge. Adversity can be a powerful partner in learning new skills and achieving success in the future. Life is best lived as an adventure, with never-ending wonder and delight at the heart of its many challenges.

FINAL THOUGHTS

The intent of this book was to provide a venue for student affairs educators to share their inspirational and humorous stories along with any lessons they learned. The stories are both personal and anecdotal, providing glimpses into the lives of student affairs professionals. Intentionally, this book does not connect with the literature. It is neither a scholarly work nor a reference text. Rather, it is meant to be a collection of uplifting essays, conversations, and poems that can provide the needed reinforcement for anyone who might have lost sight of the rewards of this profession.

Staying motivated in student affairs is not easy. As Jon Dalton reminds us, "Certainly one of the most important challenges of professional success and fulfillment is how to continually renew one's energies and commitment. Burnout and boredom are not so much the consequences of doing the same things over and over again as they are the failure to recharge one's spirit and enthusiasms" (quoted in Reisser, 2002, p. 50). These stories offer inspiration and encouragement for anyone who requires a recharge of the spirit.

The narratives, written by authors from every level of practice, allow us to learn from the experiences of others and challenge us to identify lessons that may improve our practice. These testimonials are intended to help those in the student affairs profession by reinforcing the significant role we play on college campuses, teaching us valuable lessons, and simply helping us laugh. This is the kind of book that I hope professors will assign for those beginning their careers in student affairs, mentors will give to mentees, and inexperienced and seasoned professionals alike will read for pleasure.

Although *Stories of Inspiration* was intended for individual consumption, it may also be used in the classroom, in professional development workshops, or as a springboard for conversation on the significance of student affairs work. These stories may serve several purposes. First, they can awaken us to our potential. Often, the work of student affairs is not quantifiable and is even devalued on our campuses. These narratives serve as validation for us and our profession. They make us proud of the positive impact we have on the lives of students. These anecdotes remind us that even "the briefest interaction, dealing with what appears to be the most mundane issue, can have tremendous impact on the person to whom that issue matters most" (Roper, 2002, p. 12).

Second, many of the stories are excellent examples of practical wisdom that can be used in the classroom or the practitioner arena. As defined by Dalton (2002), practical wisdom includes the successful combination of sound knowledge and good judgment. Practical wisdom involves the "ability to draw upon knowledge selectively and apply it successfully in specific situations" (Dalton, 2002, p. 3). One of the key resources for learning practical wisdom is sharing within a community of professional colleagues. Reading these stories is an excellent way for colleagues to learn from one another. Admittedly, not all stories represent perfection. Indeed, student affairs educators can be fallible, but these authors are willing to learn from their mistakes. They impart their wisdom with the hope that others may learn from their experiences.

Third, this book may be used in the classroom to help inform new or incipient professionals. Through story, the diversity of our work is explored, along with a deeper understanding of the impact of student affairs work on both students and professionals. One may also use some of the narratives to apply student development theory. For example, some of the accounts that focus on students and their experiences nicely demonstrate the delicate balance between challenge and support (Sanford, 1962), while others reinforce the ideas outlined in Alexander Astin's involvement theory (1984) or Nancy Schlossberg's mattering and marginality (1989). Some of the stories may be connected to Arthur Chickering and Linda Reisser's vectors of development (1993); the ones involving student discipline may be analyzed using the lens of Lawrence Kohlberg's theory of moral development (1975).

Last, many of these stories serve as reminders that we cannot take ourselves too seriously. We know our work is not easy and often is challenging. Laughter can get us through the difficult times. As Larry Roper says, "Laughter and humor provide a vehicle for maintaining a positive perspective" (quoted in Reisser, 2002, p. 55). May the humorous stories in this book bring a smile to your face and assist you in maintaining a positive outlook.

Use these stories as case studies, examples of practical wisdom, points of laughter, or sources of renewal. Remember that as student affairs educators, we all have stories to tell. I hope that reading this book encourages you to share your own stories with colleagues, students, parents, supervisors—anyone who will listen. Storytelling allows us to celebrate our successes, learn from our mistakes, and renew our commitment to our vocation. Stories can rekindle a passion and make the idea of "making a difference" irresistible. Student affairs men and women encourage, enlighten, challenge, and inspire students every day. Let us make certain that these stories are told and retold as we strive to validate our presence on campus and demonstrate the significant impact we have on the education of our students.

References

Astin, A. W. (1984). Student involvement: A developmental theory for higher education. *Journal of College Student Personnel,* 25, 297-308.

Chickering, A. W., & Reisser, L. (1993). *Education and identity* (2nd ed.). San Francisco: Jossey-Bass.

Dalton, J. (2002). The art and practical wisdom of student affairs leadership. In J. Dalton & M. McClinton (Eds.), *The art and practical wisdom of student affairs leadership* (New Directions for Student Services, No. 98, pp. 3-10). San Francisco: Jossey-Bass.

Kohlberg, L. (1975). *The cognitive-developmental approach to moral education.* Phi Delta Kappan, 56, 670-677.

Reisser, L. (2002). Self-renewal and personal development in professional life. In J. Dalton & M. McClinton (Eds.), *The art and practical wisdom of student affairs leadership* (New Directions for Student Services, No. 98, pp. 49-60). San Francisco: Jossey-Bass.

Roper, L. (2002). Relationships: The critical ties that bind professionals. In J. Dalton & M. McClinton (Eds.), *The art and practical wisdom of student affairs leadership* (New Directions for Student Services, No. 98, pp. 11-26). San Francisco: Jossey-Bass.

Sanford, N. (1962). *The American college.* New York: Wiley.

Schlossberg, N. K. (1989).Marginality and mattering: Key issues in building community. In D. C. Roberts (Ed.) *Designing campus activities to foster a sense of community* (New Directions for Student Services No. 48, pp 5-15). San Francisco: Jossey-Bass.

AFTERWARD

Have a story to share? Please forward it to Sarah M. Marshall, Ph.D., at sarah.marshall@cmich.edu. The story may be considered for future publication.

ACKNOWLEDGMENTS

I thank NASPA for publishing this unique collection of stories. I am grateful for the commitment to publishing pieces that inform our profession in the form of scholarship, best practices, and, in this case, creative endeavors.

I would like to thank the story contributors for their willingness to share their personal experiences with the profession. You have inspired us, made us laugh, and helped renew our sense of purpose. Your genuine stories, told from the heart, help us better understand the impact of student affairs and reinforce our commitment to the field.

Last, I thank my family for bringing joy and inspiration to my life every day. I thank my parents for believing in me and instilling in me the belief that anything is possible. Thank you to my husband and children for loving me unconditionally and for the daily reminder of what really matters in my life.

CONTRIBUTING AUTHORS

SARAH M. MARSHALL, PH.D., is an assistant professor of educational administration and community leadership at Central Michigan University. She also served as a faculty member in higher education administration at Oklahoma State University and a hall director, assistant director of residence life, and director of student activities. She earned her Ph.D. in higher education administration and M.Ed. in college student personnel at Loyola University, Chicago. Her B.A. is in Spanish and economics from Albion College.

C. RYAN AKERS, a NASPA student member, is a Ph.D. candidate in student affairs administration at the University of Georgia. He received a B.S. in biology and a B.A. in psychology from Delta State University and an M.S. in counselor education from Mississippi State University.

LEE E. BIRD, PH.D., is the vice president for student affairs at Oklahoma State University. She holds a B.S. in education from the University of Arizona, an M.S. in counseling and guidance from the University of Wisconsin, and a Ph.D. in higher education from the University of Arizona.

ELIZABETH BALDIZAN, ED.D., received her Ed.D. in higher educational administration from the University of Nevada, Las Vegas, her M.A. in education from the University of New Mexico, and her B.A. in communications and environmental studies from the University of Northern Colorado. Dr. Baldizan served as the assistant dean of students at the University of New Mexico, dean of student life at South Seattle Community College, and dean of student development at UNLV. She has served on the NASPA Board of Directors.

HEATH P. BOICE-PARDEE, ED.D., is the assistant dean for new student programs at Rutgers College. A student affairs educator with over 12 years of professional experience, he holds a master's in education and counseling from the College of St. Rose in Albany, N.Y., and a doctorate in education from Rutgers.

SCOTT C. BROWN, PH.D., is the director of the Daniel L. Jones Career Development Center and an adjunct lecturer in the department of psychology and education at Mount Holyoke College, and has held posts at the University of Maryland (Ph.D.), American Association for Higher Education, Dartmouth College, Semester at Sea, Indiana University (M.S.), and the University of California, Irvine (B.A.).

WILLIAM B. BYNUM JR., PH.D., is the vice president for student affairs and enrollment management at Lincoln University. Dr. Bynum earned his bachelor of arts degree in sociology at Davidson College and his master's and Ph.D. in sociology from Duke University.

JAY R. COOPER, ED.D., served as editor of the Idlers of the Bamboo Grove for three years. He earned a B.S. from Oakland University, an M.S.Ed. from Southern Illinois University, and his Ed.D. from Western Michigan University. He has worked in student affairs for 20 years at SIU, the University of South Carolina, Columbia, and Grand Valley State University. He has served the last three years as a faculty member in the College Student Affairs Leadership Program at Grand Valley State University.

BOB CROW is dean of student development at Calvin College. He was dean of students at Malone College. His undergraduate degree came from Grove City College and his M.A. from Slippery Rock University.

CLIFFORD E. DENAY JR. holds a master's degree in counseling and a specialist in education degree from Central Michigan University. He is a licensed professional counselor and adjunct professor of psychology at North Central Michigan College. His articles have appeared in such publications as *Psychology for Living, Men of Integrity, The War Cry,* and several others.

GYPSY M. DENZINE, PH.D., is the associate dean in the College of Education at Northern Arizona University. She also is an associate professor of educational psychology. She earned her doctoral degree from the University of Northern Colorado in educational psychology.

ROBERT E. DIXON, ED.D., has served in various administrative positions in higher education at Mercer University and Oklahoma State University. He currently serves as director of grants and contracts financial administration at Oklahoma State. He is active in the Southern Association of College and University Business Officers.

FELICE DUBLON, PH.D., is the vice president and dean of student affairs at the School of the Art Institute of Chicago. She is a past president of the Association for Student Judicial Affairs. She serves on the editorial board of the NASPA *Journal*. Dr. Dublon earned bachelor's degrees in psychology and political science and a master's degree in counseling psychology from the University of Illinois. She earned her Ph.D. in higher education administration from Florida State University.

SHANNON ELLIS, PH.D., is the vice president for student services at the University of Nevada, Reno. She has worked in higher education for more than 25 years. Dr. Ellis received her Ph.D. from the University of Southern California in higher education and law, her master's from the University of Massachusetts in public administration, and her B.S. from the University of Illinois-Champaign/Urbana in journalism. She has served as the president of NASPA and recently published *Dreams, Nightmares and Pursuing the Passion: Reflections on Leadership in Higher Education.*

JENNIFER FONSECA was formerly the Director of the First Year Experience program at Palm Beach Atlantic University. She received her master of education degree from the University of Toledo and her bachelor of science degree in journalism from Bowling Green State University.

TROY GILBERT has a B.A. and an M.S. in higher education and student affairs from Indiana University Bloomington. His experience includes working in residence life at California Polytechnic, San Luis Obispo; student leadership and activities at Stanford University; and corporate human resources at Gap, Inc. (Gap, Banana Republic, Old Navy). He is the associate director of the Office of Student Development at the University of California, Berkeley.

ROBERT GLENN, PH.D., completed his undergraduate work at Birmingham-Southern College and his master's and doctorate at the University of Alabama in counselor education. Prior to his current position as vice president for student affairs and vice provost for enrollment and academic services at Middle Tennessee State University, Dr. Glenn held student affairs positions at Missouri State University, the University of North Alabama, and Birmingham-Southern College.

THOMAS J. GRITES, PH.D., is assistant to the provost at Stockton College. He earned his B.A. and M.A. degrees in education from Illinois State University and his Ph.D. in counseling and personnel services from the University of Maryland, College Park. He was a founding member of the National Academic Advising Association and was its second president. He has published, presented, and consulted on the topic of academic advising in higher education.

GAIL SHORT HANSON, PH.D., is the vice president of campus life at American University in Washington, D.C. Dr. Hanson is a past president of the National Association for Women in Education. She is on the Board of Directors of Susquehanna University and on NASPA's Advisory Board for the Center for Scholarship, Research, and Professional Development for Women. Dr. Hanson earned her B.A. from the University of Wisconsin. She also holds an M.Ed. and an M.Phil. and Ph.D. in sociology from George Washington University.

JIM D. HARDWICK, ED.D., a 20-year practitioner in student affairs, is the vice president for student life at Carroll College. He was the dean of students at St. John's University and the associate director of campus programs and organizations at Albion College. Dr. Hardwick has his doctorate in educational policy and administration from the University of Minnesota, his master's of education in counselor education from North Dakota State University, and a bachelor of science in management and political science from Minnesota State University Moorhead.

PEGGY C. HOLZWEISS serves as the assessment coordinator in the Department of Student Life Studies at Texas A&M University. She has a bachelor's degree in psychology and a master's degree in student affairs administration from Texas A&M. She served on the Bonfire Advisory Committee for three years while working in the student union. She has been in the field for more than 10 years.

HEATH HUBER is the program manager of Bowling Green State University's Wood County Corps, an AmeriCorps program. He served as the community educator of the Transformation Project of the BGSU Women's Center. He holds a master's degree in college student personnel from BGSU, co-chairs BGSU's Coalition Against Sexual Offenses, and trains the campus and community on issues regarding violence.

CAROL A. LUNDBERG, PH.D., earned her Ph.D. in higher education from Claremont Graduate University and her M.A. in student development from Azusa Pacific University. Prior to working as a faculty member in the Department of Higher Education and Organizational Leadership at Azusa Pacific, she coordinated new student orientation and leadership programs at Westmont College and at California State University, San Bernardino.

KEN LYNDY graduated from Wilmington College with a B.A. in theater and criminal justice. He holds an M.Ed. in student affairs administration from Wright State University. After starting his professional career in housing, he has been employed as the director of student activities at Wilmington.

ANN MARIE MALLOY has been on the arts and humanities faculty of Tulsa Community College for 17 years. She has a B.A. in letters from the University of Oklahoma and an M.A. in modern humanities from the University of Tulsa. She is a doctoral student in educational leadership at Oklahoma State University.

MELINDA MANNING, J.D., is the assistant dean of students at the University of North Carolina, Chapel Hill. She received a B.A. in history and political science as well as a J.D. from the University of North Carolina at Chapel Hill. She spent three years teaching middle school as a part of the Teach for America program in rural Mississippi.

CARRIE E. MEYER has a bachelor of arts in psychology from Adrian College and a master's degree in student affairs administration from Western Michigan University. She works as Director of Student Activities at Flagler College.

MINDY MICHELS, PH.D., is the director of the American University Gay, Lesbian, Bisexual, Transgender and Ally Resource Center. She earned her B.A. from the University of California, Los Angelas and her Ph.D. in anthropology from American University.

BECCA MINTON received her M.S. in student affairs administration from Texas A&M University. She now serves Texas A&M as a student development specialist. Prior to attending graduate school, Becca taught elementary music in Austin. She received a B.S. in instrumental music education from Northwest Missouri State University.

BOB MOSIER, PH.D., is the former director of residential living at the University of Wisconsin–Stevens Point, and is the current co-coordinator of UWSP's self-study process. He earned his B.A. from The College of New Jersey, his M.A. from the University of Illinois, and his Ph.D. from Ohio State University. Bob served as president of the Association of College and University Housing Officers-International (ACUHO-I) and as editor of its *Journal of College and University Student Housing*.

WILLIAM E. O'DELL graduated from Central Michigan University with a bachelor's degree in English and history. He was an area coordinator for residential housing, then moved into private and corporate retail before deciding to go back into higher education. O'Dell works for Central Michigan University as a residence hall director. He is working toward his master's degree in education with an emphasis in student affairs.

KRIS OLDS has been a hall director for five and a half years. She has a degree in applied psychology with an emphasis in counseling from St. Cloud State University.

MONICA PARIKH is a doctoral student in higher education administration at the University at Buffalo, where she completed her master's degree. She currently holds an assistantship in the office of admissions.

KEVIN POLLOCK, PH.D., received his Ph.D. in higher, adult, and lifelong education from Michigan State University. His writings are included in the *SEM Anthology* and *Essentials of Enrollment Management: Cases in the Field*. He is vice president of student services at West Shore Community College.

LINDA R. QUALIA, PH.D., directs the counseling services at Collin County Community College. Dr. Qualia received her Ph.D. in counselor education from the University of North Texas, her M.A. in psychology from the University of Alabama, and her B.A. in psychology from Rhodes College.

LORI REESOR, PH.D., is an associate dean and assistant professor in the School of Education at the University of Missouri–Kansas City. She was the dean of students at Wichita State University. She has her doctorate from the University of Kansas, a master's degree from Iowa State University, and a bachelor's degree from the University of Wisconsin, Whitewater.

JAMES RHATIGAN, PH.D., was the vice president for student affairs and dean of students and then senior vice president at Wichita State University before he retired in 2002. Since then, he has been a consultant to the WSU Foundation. He has held a number of positions in NASPA, including historian and president. He received his Ph.D. in college personnel administration from the University of Iowa.

TIMOTHY D. SHAAL is a residence hall director at Bowling Green State University. He received his master of science degree in counseling from Shippensburg University. He was an undergraduate R.A. and has worked at several institutions in residence life.

LINDA TIMM, PH.D., is the vice president for student affairs at St. Mary's College. Summer 2006 she will assume the presidency of Mount Mary College in Milwaukee, Wis.. Dr. Timm holds a bachelor's degree in communication, a master's degree in education, and a doctorate in educational administration and foundations from Illinois State University. For the Association for Student

Judicial Affairs, she served as the founding secretary, program chairperson, and president. She is a member of the Board of Directors of the Association for Student Affairs at Catholic Colleges and Universities.

KATY VENCE is an alumnus of Bowling Green State University. She served as a Peace Corps volunteer in South Africa and is currently an elementary school teacher.

WANDA L.E. VIENTO is currently finishing her Ph.D. in student affairs in higher education at Western Michigan University, where she was the coordinator of LBG Student Services and taught classes in race and culture in the social work department. Currently, she is the coordinator of the Boise State University Women's Center.

JANET E. WALBERT, PH.D., is the vice president for student affairs and dean of students at Arcadia University and previously served in student affairs positions at Lehigh University, LaSalle University, and Drexel University. She has an Ed.D. from Lehigh University, an M.Ed. from the University of Vermont, and a B.A. from Juniata College.

DIANE WARYOLD, PH.D., is an assistant professor of human development and psychological counseling at Appalachian State University. She served as the executive director for the Center for Academic Integrity and program administrator for the Kenan Institute for Ethics at Duke University. She is a charter member of the Association for Student Judicial Affairs. Dr. Waryold received a B.S. from the State University College at Cortland, N.Y., an M.Ed. from the University of Florida, and a Ph.D. in educational leadership from Florida State University.